The Chances by John Fletcher

John Fletcher was born in December, 1579 in Rye, Sussex. He was baptised on December 20th.

As can be imagined details of much of his life and career have not survived and, accordingly, only a very brief indication of his life and works can be given.

Young Fletcher appears at the very young age of eleven to have entered Corpus Christi College at Cambridge University in 1591. There are no records that he ever took a degree but there is some small evidence that he was being prepared for a career in the church.

However what is clear is that this was soon abandoned as he joined the stream of people who would leave University and decamp to the more bohemian life of commercial theatre in London.

The upbringing of the now teenage Fletcher and his seven siblings now passed to his paternal uncle, the poet and minor official Giles Fletcher. Giles, who had the patronage of the Earl of Essex may have been a liability rather than an advantage to the young Fletcher. With Essex involved in the failed rebellion against Elizabeth Giles was also tainted.

By 1606 John Fletcher appears to have equipped himself with the talents to become a playwright. Initially this appears to have been for the Children of the Queen's Revels, then performing at the Blackfriars Theatre.

Fletcher's early career was marked by one significant failure; The Faithful Shepherdess, his adaptation of Giovanni Battista Guarini's Il Pastor Fido, which was performed by the Blackfriars Children in 1608.

By 1609, however, he had found his stride. With his collaborator John Beaumont, he wrote Philaster, which became a hit for the King's Men and began a profitable association between Fletcher and that company. Philaster appears also to have begun a trend for tragicomedy.

By the middle of the 1610s, Fletcher's plays had achieved a popularity that rivalled Shakespeare's and cemented the pre-eminence of the King's Men in Jacobean London. After his frequent early collaborator John Beaumont's early death in 1616, Fletcher continued working, both singly and in collaboration, until his own death in 1625. By that time, he had produced, or had been credited with, close to fifty plays.

Index of Contents

DRAMATIS PERSONAE
MEN
Duke of Ferrara.
Petruchio, Governour of Bolognia.
Don John,   } two Spanish Gentlemen, and Comerades.
Don Frederick,   }
Antonio, an old stout Gentleman, Kinsman to Petruchio.
Three Gentlemen, friends to the Duke.
Two Gentlemen, friends to Petruchio.
Francisco, a Musician, Antonio's Boy.
Peter Vecchio, a Teacher of Latine
and Musick, a reputed Wizard.
Peter &   } two Servants to Don John and Frederick.
Anthony   }
A Surgeon
WOMEN
Constancia, Sister to Petruchio, and Mistriss to the Duke.
Gentlewoman, Servant to Constancia.
Old Gentlewoman, Landlady to Don John and Frederick.
Constancia, a Whore to old Antonio.

Bawd.

THE SCENE: Bolognia

PROLOGUE

Aptness for Mirth to all, this instant Night
Thalia hath prepared for your delight,
Her Choice and curious Viands, in each part
Season'd with rarities of Wit and Art;
Nor fear I to be tax'd for a vain boast,
My Promise will find Credit with the most,
When they know ingenious Fletcher made it, he
Being in himself a perfect Comedie:
And some sit here, I doubt not, dare averr
Living he made that House a Theatre
Which he pleas'd to frequent; and thus much we
Could not but pay to his lovd Memorie.
For our selves, we do entreat that you would not
Expect strange turns, and windings in the Plot,
Objects of State, and now and then a Rhime,
To gall particular Persons with the time;
Or that his towring Muse hath made her flight
Nearer your apprehension than your sight;
But if that sweet Expressions, quick Conceit,
Familiar Language, fashion'd to the weight
Of such as speak it, have the power to raise
Your Grace to us, with Trophies to his Praise;
We may profess, presuming on his Skill,
If his Chances please not you, our Fortune's ill.

ACTUS PRIMUS

SCÆNA PRIMA

Enter Two Serving-men, **PETER** and **ANTHONY**.

PETER
I would we were remov'd from this town, Anthony,
That we might taste some quiet; for mine own part,
I'm almost melted with continual trotting
After enquiries, dreams, and revelations,
Of who knows whom, or where? serve wenching soldiers,

That knows no other Paradise but Plackets:
I'll serve a Priest in Lent first, and eat Bell-ropes.

ANTHONY
Thou art the froward'st fool—

PETER
Why, good tame Anthonie?
Tell me but this; to what end came we hither?

ANTHONY
To wait upon our Masters.

PETER
But how, Anthony?
Answer me that; resolve me there, good Anthony?

ANTHONY
To serve their uses.

PETER
Shew your uses, Anthony.

ANTHONY
To be imploy'd in any thing.

PETER
No Anthony,
Not any thing I take it; nor that thing
We travel to discover, like new islands;
A salt itch serve such uses; in things of moment
Concerning things, I grant ye, not things errant,
Sweet Ladies things, and things to thank the Surgeon;
In no such things, sweet Anthony, put case—

ANTHONY
Come, come, all will be mended; this invisible woman
Of infinite report for shape and vertue,
That bred us all this trouble to no purpose,
They are determin'd now no more to think on,
But fall close to their studies.

PETER
Was there ever
Men known to run mad with report before?
Or wonder after that they know not where
To find? or if found, how to enjoy? are mens brains
Made now adays of malt, that their affections

Are never sober? but like drunken People
Founder at every new Fame? I do believe too
That men in love are ever drunk, as drunken men
Are ever loving.

ANTHONY
Prithee be thou sober,
And know, that they are none of those, not guilty
Of the least vanity of love, only a doubt
Fame might too far report, or rather flatter
The Graces of this Woman, made them curious
To find the truth, which since they find so blocked
And lockt up from their searches, they are now setled
To give the wonder over.

PETER
Would they were setled
To give me some new shoos too: for I'll be sworn
These are e'en worn out to the reasonable souls
In their good worships business; and some sleep
Would not do much amiss, unless they mean
To make a Bell-man on me; and what now
Mean they to study, Anthony, moral Philosophy
After their mar-all women?

ANTHONY
Mar a fools head.

PETER
'Twill mar two fools heads and they take not heed,
Besides the Giblets to 'em.

ANTHONY
Will you walk, Sir,
And talk more out of hearing? your fools head
May chance to find a wooden night-cap else.

PETER
I never lay in any.

[Enter **DON JOHN** and **FREDERICK**.

ANTHONY
Then leave your lying,
And your blind prophesying: here they come,
You had best tell them as much.

PETER

I am no tell-tale.

[Exeunt.

DON JOHN
I would we could have seen her though; for sure
She must be some rare Creature, or Report lies.
All mens Reports too.

FREDERICK
I could well wish I had seen her;
But since she is so conceal'd, so beyond venture
Kept and preserv'd from view, so like a Paradise,
Plac'd where no knowledge can come near her; so guarded,
As 'twere impossible, though known, to reach her,
I have made up my belief.

DON JOHN
Hang me from this hour
If I more think upon her, or believe her,
But as she came a strong Report unto me,
So the next Fame shall lose her.

FREDERICK
'Tis the next way;
But whither are you walking?

DON JOHN
My old Round
After my meat, and then to Bed.

FREDERICK
'Tis healthful.

DON JOHN
Will not you stir?

FREDERICK
I have a little business.

DON JOHN
Upon my life this Lady still—

FREDERICK
Then you will lose it.

DON JOHN
'Pray let's walk together.

FREDERICK
Now I cannot.

DON JOHN
I have something to impart.

FREDERICK
An hour hence
I will not miss to meet you.

DON JOHN
Where?

FREDERICK
I'th' high street;
For not to lie, I have a few Devotions
To do first, then I am yours.

DON JOHN
Remember.

[Exeunt.

SCÆNA SECUNDA

Enter **PETRUCHIO, ANTONIO**, and **TWO GENTLEMEN**.

ANTONIO
Cut his wind-pipe I say.

FIRST GENTLEMEN
Fye, Antonio.

ANTONIO
Or knock his brains out first, and then forgive him,
If you do thrust, be sure it be to th'hilts,
A Surgeon may see through him.

FIRST GENTLEMEN
You are too violent.

SECOND GENTLEMEN
Too open undiscreet.

PETER

Am I not ruin'd?
The honour of my house crack'd? my bloud poyson'd?
My Credit and my Name?

SECOND GENTLEMEN
Be sure it be so,
Before ye use this violence: Let not doubt,
And a suspecting anger so much sway ye,
Your wisedom may be question'd.

ANTONIO
I say kill him,
And then dispute the cause; cut off what may be,
And what is shall be safe.

SECOND GENTLEMEN
Hang up a true man,
Because 'tis possible he may be thievish!
Alas, is this good Justice?

PETER
I know as certain
As day must come again, as clear as truth,
And open as belief can lay it to me,
That I am basely wrong'd, wrong'd above recompence;
Maliciously abus'd, blasted for ever
In name and honour, lost to all remembrance,
But what is smear'd, and shameful; I must kill him,
Necessity compells me.

FIRST GENTLEMEN
But think better.

PETER
There is no other cure left; yet witness with me,
All that is fair in man, all that is noble,
I am not greedy of this life I seek for,
Nor thirst to shed mans blood, and would 'twere possible,
I wish it with my soul, so much I tremble
To offend the sacred Image of my Maker,
My Sword could only kill his Crimes; no, 'tis Honour,
Honour, my noble friends, that Idol, Honour,
That all the world now worships, not Petruchio
Must do this Justice.

ANTONIO
Let it once be done,
And 'tis no matter, whether you, or honour,

Or both, be accessary.

SECOND GENTLEMEN
Do you weigh, Petruchio,
The value of the person, power, and greatness,
And what this spark may kindle?

PETER
To perform it,
So much I am ty'd to Reputation,
And Credit of my house, let it raise wild-fires,
That all this Dukedom smoak, and storms that toss me
Into the waves of everlasting ruine,
Yet I must through; if ye dare side me.

ANTONIO
Dare?

PETER
Y'are friends indeed, if not.

SECOND GENTLEMEN
Here's none flyes from you,
Do it in what design ye please, we'll back ye.

FIRST GENTLEMEN
But then be sure ye kill him.

SECOND GENTLEMEN
Is the cause
So mortal, nothing but his life?

PETER
Believe me,
A less offence has been the desolation
Of a whole name.

SECOND GENTLEMEN
No other way to purge it?

PETER
There is, but never to be hoped for.

SECOND GENTLEMEN
Think an hour more,
And if then ye find no safer Road to guide ye,
We'll set up our Rests too.

ANTONIO
Mine's up already,
And hang him for my part
Goes less than life.

SECOND GENTLEMEN
If we see noble cause, 'tis like our Swords
May be as free and forward as your words.

[Exeunt.

SCÆNA TERTIA

Enter **DON JOHN**.

DON JOHN
The civil order of this Town, Bologna,
Makes it belov'd and honour'd of all Travellers,
As a most safe retirement in all troubles;
Beside the wholsome seat, and noble temper
Of those minds that inhabit it, safely wise,
And to all strangers vertuous; But I see
My admiration has drawn night upon me,
And longer to expect my friend may pull me
Into suspicion of too late a stirrer,
Which all good Governments are jealous of.
I'll home, and think at liberty: yet certain,
'Tis not so far night as I thought; for see,
A fair house yet stands open, yet all about it
Are close, and no lights stirring, there may be foul play;
I'le venture to look in: if there be knaves,
I may do a good office.

WOMAN [within]
Signieur?

DON JOHN
What? how is this?

WOMAN WITHIN
Signieur Fabritio?

DON JOHN
I'le go nearer.

WOMAN WITHIN

Fabritio?

DON JOHN
This is a womans tongue, here may be good done.

WOMAN WITHIN
Who's there?
Fabritio?

DON JOHN
I.

WOMAN WITHIN
Where are ye?

DON JOHN
Here.

WOMAN WITHIN
O come, for Heavens sake!

DON JOHN
I must see what this means.

[Enter **WOMAN** with a **CHILD**.

WOMAN
I have stay'd this long hour for you, make no noise,
For things are in strange trouble: here, be secret,
'Tis worth your care; begon now; more eyes watch us,
Than may be for our safeties.

DON JOHN
Hark ye?

WOMAN
Peace: good night.

DON JOHN
She is gone, and I am loaden; fortune for me;
It weighs well, and it feels well; it may chance
To be some pack of worth: byth' mass 'tis heavie;
If it be Coyn or Jewels, 'tis worth welcom:
I'le ne're refuse a fortune: I am confident
'Tis of no common price: now to my lodging:
If it hit right, I'le bless this night.

[Exit.

SCÆNA QUARTA

Enter **FREDERICK**.

FREDERICK
'Tis strange,
I cannot meet him; sure he has encountred
Some light o' love or other, and there means
To play at in and in for this night. Well Don John,
If you do spring a leak, or get an itch,
Till ye claw off your curl'd pate, thank your night-walks:
You must be still a bootehalling: one round more,
Though it be late, I'le venture to discover ye,
I do not like your out-leaps.

[Exit.

SCÆNA QUINTA

Enter **DUKE** and **THREE GENTLEMEN**.

DUKE
Welcom to Town, are ye all fit?

FIRST GENTLEMEN
To point Sir.

DUKE
Where are the horses?

SECOND GENTLEMEN
Where they were appointed.

DUKE
Be private, and whatsoever fortune
Offer it self, let's stand sure.

THIRD GENTLEMEN
Fear not us,
E're ye shall be endangered, or deluded,
We'll make a black night on't.

DUKE

No more, I know it;
You know your Quarters?

FIRST GENTLEMEN
Will you go alone Sir?

DUKE
Ye shall not be far from me, the least noise
Shall bring ye to my rescue.

SECOND GENTLEMEN
We are counsell'd.

[Exeunt.

SCÆNA SEXTA

Enter **DON JOHN**.

DON JOHN
Was ever man so paid for being curious?
Ever so bob'd for searching out adventures,
As I am? did the Devil lead me? must I needs be peeping
Into mens houses where I had no business,
And make my self a mischief? 'Tis well carried;
I must take other mens occasions on me,
And be I know not whom: most finely handled:
What have I got by this now? what's the purchase?
A piece of evening Arras work, a child,
Indeed an Infidel: this comes of peeping:
A lump got out of laziness; good white bread
Let's have no bawling with ye: 'sdeath, have I
Known wenches thus long, all the ways of wenches
Their snares and subtilties? have I read over
All their School learnings, div'd into their quiddits,
And am I now bum-fidled with a Bastard?
Fetch'd over with a Card of five, and in mine old days,
After the dire massacre of a million
Of Maiden-heads? caught the common way, i'th' night too
Under anothers name, to make the matter
Carry more weight about it? well Don John,
You will be wiser one day, when ye have purchas'd
A heavy of these Butter-prints together,
With searching out conceal'd iniquities,
Without commission: why, it would never grieve me,
If I had got this Ginger-bread: never stirr'd me,

So I had had a stroak for't: 't had been Justice
Then to have kept it; but to raise a dayrie
For other mens adulteries, consume my self in candles,
And scowring works, in Nurses Bells and Babies,
Only for charity, for meer I thank you,
A little troubles me: the least touch for it,
Had but my breeches got it, had contented me.
Whose e're it is, sure 't had a wealthy Mother,
For 'tis well cloathed, and if I be not cozen'd,
Well lin'd within: to leave it here were barbarous,
And ten to one would kill it: a more sin
Then his that got it: well, I will dispose on't,
And keep it, as they keep deaths heads in rings,
To cry memento to me; no more peeping.
Now all the danger is to qualifie
The good old gentlewoman, at whose house we live,
For she will fall upon me with a Catechism
Of four hours long: I must endure all;
For I will know this Mother: Come good wonder,
Let you and I be jogging: your starv'd trebble
Will waken the rude watch else: all that be
Curious night-walkers, may they find my fee.

[Exit.

SCÆNA SEPTIMA

Enter **FREDERICK**.

FREDERICK
Sure he's gone home:
I have beaten all the purlews,
But cannot bolt him: if he be a bobbing,
'Tis not my care can cure him: To morrow morning
I shall have further knowledge from a Surgeon's—
Where he lyes moor'd, to mend his leaks.

[Enter **CONSTANTIA**.

CONSTANTIA
I'm ready,
And through a world of dangers am flown to ye.
Be full of haste and care, we are undone else:
Where are your people? which way must we travel?
For Heaven sake stay not here Sir.

FREDERICK
What may this prove?

CONSTANTIA
Alas I am mistaken, lost, undone,
For ever perish'd. Sir, for Heaven sake tell me,
Are ye a Gentleman?

FREDERICK
I am.

CONSTANTIA
Of this place?

FREDERICK
No, born in Spain.

CONSTANTIA
As ever you lov'd honour,
As ever your desires may gain their ends,
Do a poor wretched woman but this benefit,
For I am forc'd to trust ye.

FREDERICK
Y'ave charm'd me,
Humanity and honour bids me help ye;
And if I fail your trust.—

CONSTANTIA
The time's too dangerous
To stay your protestations: I believe ye,
Alas, I must believe ye: From this place,
Good noble Sir, remove me instantly,
And for a time, where nothing but your self,
And honest conversation may come near me,
In some secure place settle me: what I am
And why thus boldly I commit my credit
Into a strangers hand, the fears and dangers,
That force me to this wild course, at more leisure
I shall reveal unto you.

FREDERICK
Come, be hearty,
He must strike through my life that takes ye from me.

[Exeunt.

SCÆNA OCTAVIA

Enter **PETRUCHIO**, **ANTONIO** and **TWO GENTLEMEN**.

PETRUCHIO
He will sure come. Are ye well arm'd?

ANTONIO
Never fear us.
Here's that will make 'em dance without a Fiddle.

PETRUCHIO
We are to look for no weak foes, my friends,
Nor unadvised ones.

ANTONIO
Best gamesters make the best game,
We shall fight close and handsom then.

FIRST GENTLEMEN
Antonio,
You are a thought too bloudy.

ANTONIO
Why? all Physicians
And penny Almanacks allow the opening
Of veins this moneth: why do ye talk of bloudy?
What come we for, to fall to cuffes for apples?
What, would ye make the cause a Cudgel quarrel?
On what terms stands this man? is not his honour
Open'd to his hand, and pickt out like an Oyster?
His credit like a quart pot knockt together,
Able to hold no liquor? clear but this point.

PETRUCHIO
Speak softly, gentle cousin.

ANTONIO
I'le speak truly;
What should men do ally'd to these disgraces,
Lick o're his enemie, sit down, and dance him?

SECOND GENTLEMEN
You are as far o'th' bow hand now.

ANTONIO
And crie;

That's my fine boy, thou wilt do so no more child.

PETRUCHIO
Here are no such cold pities.

ANTONIO
By Saint Jaques
They shall not find me one: here's old tough Andrew,
A special friend of mine, and he but hold,
I'le strike 'em such a hornpipe: knocks I come for,
And the best bloud I light on; I profess it,
Not to scare Coster-mongers; If I lose mine own,
Mine audits cast, and farewel five and fifty.

PETER
Let's talk no longer, place your selves with silence,
As I directed ye, and when time calls us,
As ye are friends, so shew your selves.

ANTONIO
So be it.

[Exeunt.

SCÆNA NONA

Enter **DON JOHN** and his **LANDLADY**.

LANDLADY
Nay Son, if this be your regard.

DON JOHN
Good Mother.

LANDLADY
Good me no goods; your cousin, and your self
Are welcom to me, whilst you bear your selves
Like honest and true Gentlemen: Bring hither
To my house, that have ever been reputed
A Gentlewoman of a decent, and fair carriage,
And so behav'd my self—

DON JOHN
I know ye have.

LANDLADY

Bring hither, as I say, to make my name
Stink in my neighbours nostrils? your Devises,
Your Brats, got out of Alligant, and broken oaths?
Your Linsey Woolsy work, your hasty puddings?
I, foster up your filch'd iniquities?
Y'are deceiv'd in me, Sir, I am none
Of those receivers.

DON JOHN
Have I not sworn unto you,
'Tis none of mine, and shew'd you how I found it?

LANDLADY
Ye found an easie fool that let you get it,
She had better have worn pasterns.

DON JOHN
Will ye hear me?

LANDLADY
Oaths? what do you care for oaths to gain your ends,
When ye are high and pamper'd? What Saint know ye?
Or what Religion, but your purpos'd lewdness,
Is to be look'd for of ye? nay, I will tell ye,
You will then swear like accus'd Cut-purses,
As far off truth too; and lye beyond all Faulconers:
I'me sick to see this dealing.

DON JOHN
Heaven forbid Mother.

LANDLADY
Nay, I am very sick.

DON JOHN
Who waits there?

ANTHONY
Sir.

[Within.

DON JOHN
Bring down the bottle of Canary wine.

LANDLADY
Exceeding sick, Heav'n help me.

DON JOHN
Haste ye Sirrah,
I must ev'n make her drunk; nay gentle mother.

LANDLADY
Now fie upon ye, was it for this purpose
You fetch'd your evening walks for your digestions,
For this pretended holiness? no weather,
Not before day could hold ye from the Matins.
Were these your bo-peep prayers? ye'have pray'd well,
And with a learned zeal: watcht well too; your Saint
It seems was pleas'd as well: still sicker, sicker.

[Enter **ANTONY**, with a bottle of wine.

DON JOHN
There is no talking to her till I have drencht her.
Give me: here mother take a good round draught,
'Twill purge spleen from your spirits: deeper mother.

LANDLADY
I, I, son, you imagine this will mend all.

DON JOHN
All i' faith Mother.

LANDLADY
I confess the Wine
Will do his part.

DON JOHN
I'le pledge ye.

LANDLADY
But son John.

DON JOHN
I know your meaning mother; touch it once more,
Alas you look not well; take a round draught,
It warms the bloud well, and restores the colour,
And then we'll talk at large.

LANDLADY
A civil Gentleman?
A stranger? one the Town holds a good regard of?

DON JOHN
Nay I will silence thee.

LANDLADY
One that should weigh his fair name? oh, a stitch!

DON JOHN
There's nothing better for a stitch, good Mother,
Make no spare of it, as you love your health,
Mince not the matter.

LANDLADY
As I said, a Gentleman,
Lodge in my house? now heav'ns my comfort, Signior!

DON JOHN
I look'd for this.

LANDLADY
I did not think you would have us'd me thus;
A woman of my credit: one, heaven knows,
That lov'd you but too tenderly.

DON JOHN
Dear Mother,
I ever found your kindness, and acknowledge it.

LANDLADY
No, no, I am a fool to counsel ye. Where's the infant?
Come, let's see your Workmanship.

DON JOHN
None of mine, Mother,
But there 'tis, and a lusty one.

LANDLADY
Heaven bless thee,
Thou hadst a hasty making; but the best is,
'Tis many a good mans fortune: as I live
Your own eyes Signior, and the nether lip
As like ye, as ye had spit it.

DON JOHN
I am glad on't.

LANDLADY
Bless me, what things are these?

DON JOHN
I thought my labour

Was not all lost, 'tis gold, and these are jewels,
Both rich, and right I hope.

LANDLADY
Well, well son John,
I see ye are a wood-man, and can chuse
Your dear, though it be i'th' dark, all your discretion
Is not yet lost; this was well clapt aboard:
Here I am with you now; when as they say
Your pleasure comes with profit; when ye must needs do,
Do where ye may be done to, 'tis a wisedom
Becomes a young man well: be sure of one thing,
Lose not your labour and your time together,
It seasons of a fool, son, time is pretious,
Work wary whilst ye have it: since ye must traffick
Sometimes this slippery way, take sure hold Signior,
Trade with no broken Merchants, make your lading,
As you would make your rest, adventurously,
But with advantage ever.

DON JOHN
All this time Mother,
The child wants looking to, wants meat and Nurses.

LANDLADY
Now blessing o' thy care; it shall have all,
And instantly; I'le seek a Nurse my self, son;
'Tis a sweet child: ah my young Spaniard,
Take you no further care Sir.

DON JOHN
Yes of these Jewels,
I must by your leave Mother: these are yours,
To make your care the stronger: for the rest
I'le find a Master; the gold for bringing up on't,
I freely render to your charge.

LANDLADY
No more words,
Nor no more children, (good son) as you love me,
This may do well.

DON JOHN
I shall observe your Morals.
But where's Don Frederick, Mother?

LANDLADY
Ten to one

About the like adventure: he told me,
He was to find you out.

[Exit.

DON JOHN
Why should he stay thus?
There may be some ill chance in't: sleep I will not,
Before I have found him: now this woman's pleas'd,
I'le seek my friend out, and my care is eas'd.

[Exit.

Enter **DUKE** and **GENTLEMEN**.

FIRST GENTLEMEN
Believe Sir, 'tis as possible to do it,
As to remove the City; the main faction
Swarm through the streets like hornets, arm'd with angers
Able to ruine States: no safety left us,
Nor means to dye like men, if instantly
You draw not back again.

DUKE
May he be drawn
And quarter'd too, that turns now; were I surer
Of death than thou art of thy fears, and with death
More than those fears are too.

FIRST GENTLEMEN
Sir, I fear not.

DUKE
I would not crack my vow, start from my honour,
Because I may find danger; wound my soul,
To keep my body safe.

FIRST GENTLEMEN
I speak not Sir,
Out of a baseness to you.

DUKE
No, nor do not
Out of a baseness leave me: what is danger,

More than the weakness of our apprehensions?
A poor cold part o'th' bloud? who takes it hold of?
Cowards, and wicked livers: valiant minds
Were made the Masters of it: and as hearty Sea-men
In desperate storms, stem with a little Rudder
The tumbling ruines of the Ocean:
So with their cause and swords do they do dangers.
Say we were sure to dye all in this venture,
As I am confident against it: is there any
Amongst us of so fat a sense, so pamper'd,
Would chuse luxuriously to lye a bed,
And purge away his spirit, send his soul out
In Sugar-sops, and Syrups? Give me dying
As dying ought to be, upon mine enemy,
Parting with man-kind, by a man that's manly:
Let 'em be all the world, and bring along
Cain's envy with 'em, I will on.

SECOND GENTLEMEN
You may Sir,
But with what safety?

FIRST GENTLEMEN
Since 'tis come to dying,
You shall perceive Sir, here be those amongst us
Can dye as decently as other men,
And with as little ceremony: on brave Sir.

DUKE
That's spoken heartily.

FIRST GENTLEMEN
And he that flinches,
May he dye lowzie in a ditch.

DUKE
No more dying,
There's no such danger in it:
What's a clock?

THIRD GENTLEMEN
Somewhat above your hour.

DUKE
Away then quickly,
Make no noise, and no trouble will attend us.

[Exeunt.

SCÆNA UNDECIMA

Enter **FREDERICK** and **PETER**, with a candle.

FREDERICK
Give me the candle: so, go you out that way.

PETER
What have we now to do?

FREDERICK
And o' your life Sirrah,
Let none come near the door without my knowledge,
No not my Landlady, nor my friend.

PETER
'Tis done Sir.

FREDERICK
Nor any serious business that concerns me.

PETER
Is the wind there again?

FREDERICK
Be gone.

PETER
I am Sir.

[Exit.

[Enter **CONSTANTIA**.

FREDERICK
Now enter without fear.—And noble Lady
That safety and civility ye wish'd for
Shall truly here attend you: no rude tongue
Nor rough behaviour knows this place, no wishes
Beyond the moderation of a man,
Dare enter here; your own desires and Innocence,
Joyn'd to my vow'd obedience, shall protect you,
Were dangers more than doubts.

CONSTANTIA

Ye are truly noble,
And worth a womans trust: let it become me,
(I do beseech you, Sir) for all your kindness,
To render with my thanks, this worthless trifle;
I may be longer troublesome.

FREDERICK
Fair offices
Are still their own rewards: Heav'n bless me Lady
From selling civil courtesies: may it please ye,
If ye will force a favour to oblige me,
Draw but that cloud aside, to satisfie me
For what good Angel I am engag'd.

CONSTANTIA
It shall be,
For I am truly confident ye are honest:
The Piece is scarce worth looking on.

FREDERICK
Trust me
The abstract of all beauty, soul of sweetness;
Defend me honest thoughts, I shall grow wild else:
What eyes are there, rather what little heavens,
To stir mens contemplations! what a Paradise
Runs through each part she has! good bloud be temperate:
I must look off: too excellent an object
Confounds the sense that sees it. Noble Lady,
If there be any further service to cast on me,
Let it be worth my life, so much I honour ye,
Or the engagement of whole Families.

CONSTANTIA
Your service is too liberal, worthy Sir,
Thus far I shall entreat.

FREDERICK
Command me Lady,
You make your power too poor.

CONSTANTIA
That presently
With all convenient haste, you would retire
Unto the street you found me in.

FREDERICK
'Tis done.

CONSTANTIA
There, if you find a Gentleman opprest
With force and violence, do a mans office,
And draw your sword to rescue him.

FREDERICK
He's safe,
Be what he will, and let his foes be Devils,
Arm'd with your pity, I shall conjure 'em.
Retire, this key will guide ye: all things necessary
Are there before ye.

CONSTANTIA
All my prayers go with ye.

[Exit.

FREDERICK
Ye clap on proof upon me: men say gold
Does all, engages all, works through all dangers:
Now I say beauty can do more: The Kings Exchequer,
Nor all his wealthy Indies, could not draw me
Through half those miseries this piece of pleasure
Might make me leap into: we are all like sea-Cards,
All our endeavours and our motions,
(As they do to the North) still point at beauty,
Still at the fairest: for a handsom woman,
(Setting my soul aside) it should go hard,
But I would strain my body: yet to her,
Unless it be her own free gratitude,
Hopes ye shall dye, and thou tongue rot within me,
E're I infringe my faith: now to my rescue.

[Exit.

ACTUS SECUNDUS

SCÆNA PRIMA

Enter **DUKE**, pursued by **PETRUCHIO**, **ANTONIO** and that Faction.

DUKE
You will not all oppress me?

ANTONIO
Kill him i'th' wanton eye: let me come to him.

DUKE
Then ye shall buy me dearly.

PETRUCHIO
Say you so Sir?

ANTONIO
I say cut his Wezand, spoil his piping;
Have at your love-sick heart Sir.

[Enter **DON JOHN**.

DON JOHN
Sure 'tis fighting.
My friend may be engag'd: fie Gentlemen,
This is unmanly odds.

ANTONIO
I'le stop your mouth Sir.

[**DUKE** falls down, **DON JOHN** bestrides him.

DON JOHN
Nay, then have at thee freely:
There's a plumb Sir to satisfie your longing.

PETRUCHIO
Away: I hope I have sped him: here comes rescue,
We shall be endangered: where's Antonio?

ANTONIO
I must have one thrust more Sir.

DON JOHN
Come up to me.

ANTONIO
A mischief confound your fingers.

PETRUCHIO
How is't?

ANTONIO
Well:
Ha's given me my quietus est, I felt him
In my small guts, I'me sure, has feez'd me:
This comes of siding with ye.

SECOND GENTLEMEN
Can you go Sir?

ANTONIO
I should go man, and my head were off,
Never talk of going.

PETRUCHIO
Come, all shall be well then,
I hear more rescue coming.

[Enter the **DUKE'S FACTION**.

ANTHONY
Let's turn back then;
My skull's uncloven yet, let me but kill.

PETRUCHIO
Away for Heaven sake with him.

DON JOHN
How is't?

DUKE
Well Sir,
Only a little stagger'd.

FACTION DUKE
Let's pursue 'em.

DUKE
No not a man, I charge ye: thanks good coat,
Thou hast sav'd me a shrewd welcom: 'twas put home too,
With a good mind I'me sure on't.

DON JOHN
Are ye safe then?

DUKE
My thanks to you brave Sir, whose timely valour,
And manly courtesie came to my rescue.

DON JOHN
Ye'had foul play offer'd ye, and shame befal him
That can pass by oppression.

DUKE

May I crave Sir,
But thus much honour more, to know your name?
And him I am so bound to?

DON JOHN
For the Bond Sir,
'Tis every good mans tye: to know me further
Will little profit ye; I am a stranger,
My Country Spain; my name Don John, a Gentleman
That lye here for my study.

DUKE
I have heard Sir,
Much worthy mention of ye, yet I find
Fame short of what ye are.

DON JOHN
You are pleas'd Sir,
To express your courtesie: may I demand
As freely what you are, and what mischance
Cast you into this danger?

DUKE
For this present
I must desire your pardon: you shall know me
E're it be long Sir, and a nobler thanks
Than now my will can render.

DON JOHN
Your will's your own Sir.

DUKE
What is't you look for sir, have you lost any thing?

DON JOHN
Only my hat i'th' scuffle; sure these fellows
Were night-snaps.

DUKE
No, believe Sir: pray ye use mine,
For 'twill be hard to find your own now.

DON JOHN
No Sir.

DUKE
Indeed ye shall, I can command another:
I do beseech ye honour me.

DON JOHN
I will Sir,
And so I'le take my leave.

DUKE
Within these few days
I hope I shall be happy in your knowledge,
Till when I love your memory.

[Exit **DUKE**, &c.

DON JOHN
I yours.
This is some noble fellow.

[Enter **FREDERICK**.

FREDERICK
'Tis his tongue sure.
Don John?

DON JOHN
Don Frederick?

FREDERICK
Ye're fairly met Sir:
I thought ye had been a Bat-fowling: prethee tell me,
What Revelations hast thou had to night,
That home was never thought of?

DON JOHN
Revelations?
I'le tell thee Frederick, but before I tell thee,
Settle thy understanding.

FREDERICK
'Tis prepar'd, Sir.

DON JOHN
Why then mark what shall follow. This night Frederick,
This bawdy night.

FREDERICK
I thought no less.

DON JOHN
This blind night,

What dost think I have got?

FREDERICK
The Pox it may be.

DON JOHN
Would 'twere no worse: ye talk of Revelations,
I have got a Revelation will reveal me
An arrant Coxcomb while I live.

FREDERICK
What is't?
Thou hast lost nothing?

DON JOHN
No, I have got I tell thee.

FREDERICK
What hast thou got?

DON JOHN
One of the Infantry, a child.

FREDERICK
How?

DON JOHN
A chopping child, man.

FREDERICK
'Give ye joy, Sir.

DON JOHN
A lump of lewdness Frederick, that's the truth on't:
This Town's abominable.

FREDERICK
I still told ye John
Your whoring must come home; I counsell'd ye:
But where no grace is—

DON JOHN
'Tis none o' mine, man.

FREDERICK
Answer the Parish so.

DON JOHN

Cheated introth:
Peeping into a house, by whom I know not,
Nor where to find the place again: no Frederick,
Had I but kist the ring for't; 'tis no poor one,
That's my best comfort, for't has brought about it
Enough to make it man.

FREDERICK
Where is't?

DON JOHN
At home.

FREDERICK
A saving voyage: But what will you say Signior,
To him that searching out your serious worship,
Has met a stranger fortune?

DON JOHN
How, good Frederick?
A militant girle now to this boy would hit it?

FREDERICK
No, mine's a nobler venture: What do you think Sir
Of a distressed Lady, one whose beauty
Would oversell all Italy?

DON JOHN
Where is she—

FREDERICK
A woman of that rare behaviour,
So qualified, as admiration
Dwells round about her: of that perfect spirit—

DON JOHN
I marry Sir.

FREDERICK
That admirable carriage,
That sweetness in discourse; young as the morning,
Her blushes staining his.

DON JOHN
But where's this creature?
Shew me but that.

FREDERICK

That's all one, she's forth-coming,
I have her sure Boy.

DON JOHN
Hark ye Frederick,
What truck betwixt my Infant?

FREDERICK
'Tis too light Sir,
Stick to your charges good Don John, I am well.

DON JOHN
But is there such a wench?

FREDERICK
First tell me this,
Did ye not lately as ye walk'd along,
Discover people that were arm'd, and likely
To do offence?

DON JOHN
Yes marry, and they urg'd it
As far as they had spirit.

FREDERICK
Pray go forward.

DON JOHN
A Gentleman I found ingag'd amongst 'em,
It seems of noble breeding, I'm sure brave metal,
As I return'd to look you, I set in to him,
And without hurt (I thank heaven) rescued him,
And came my self off safe too.

FREDERICK
My work's done then:
And now to satisfie you, there is a woman,
Oh John, there is a woman—

DON JOHN
Oh, where is she?

FREDERICK
And one of no less worth than I assure ye;
And which is more, fain under my protection.

DON JOHN
I am glad of that: forward sweet Frederick.

FREDERICK
And which is more than that, by this nights wandring,
And which is most of all, she is at home too Sir.

DON JOHN
Come, let's be gone then.

FREDERICK
Yes, but 'tis most certain,
You cannot see her, John.

DON JOHN
Why?

FREDERICK
She has sworn me
That none else shall come near her: not my Mother,
Till some few doubts are clear'd.

DON JOHN
Not look upon her? What chamber is she in?

FREDERICK
In ours.

DON JOHN
Let's go I say:
A womans oaths are wafers, break with making,
They must for modestie a little: we all know it.

FREDERICK
No, I'le assure you Sir.

DON JOHN
Not see her?
I smell an old dog trick of yours, well Frederick,
Ye talkt to me of whoring, let's have fair play,
Square dealing I would wish ye.

FREDERICK
When 'tis come,
(Which I know never will be) to that issue,
Your spoon shall be as deep as mine Sir.

DON JOHN
Tell me,
And tell me true, is the cause honourable,

Or for your ease?

FREDERICK
By all our friendship, John,
'Tis honest, and of great end.

DON JOHN
I am answer'd:
But let me see her though: leave the door open
As ye go in.

FREDERICK
I dare not.

DON JOHN
Not wide open,
But just so, as a jealous husband
Would level at his wanton wife through.

FREDERICK
That courtesie,
If ye desire no more, and keep it strictly,
I dare afford ye: come, 'tis now near morning.

[Exit.

SCÆNA SECUNDA

Enter **PETER** and **ANTHONY**.

PETER
Nay the old woman's gone too.

ANTHONY
She's a Catterwauling
Among the gutters: But conceive me, Peter,
Where our good Masters should be?

PETER
Where they should be
I do conceive, but where they are, good Anthony—

ANTHONY
I, there it goes: my Masters bo-peep with me,
With his slye popping in and out again,
Argued a cause, a frippery cause.

PETER
Believe me,
They bear up with some carvel.

ANTHONY
I do believe thee,
For thou hast such a Master for that chase,
That till he spend his main Mast—

PETER
Pray remember
Your courtesie good Anthony, and withal,
How long 'tis since your Master sprung a leak,
He had a sound one since he came.

[**LUTE** sounds within.

ANTHONY
Hark.

PETER
What?

ANTHONY
Dost not hear a Lute?
Again?

PETER
Where is't?

ANTHONY
Above in my Masters chamber.

PETER
There's no creature: he hath the key himself man.

SING [within]
Merciless Love, whom nature hath deny'd
The use of eyes, lest thou should'st take a pride
And glorie in thy murthers: Why am I
That never yet transgress'd thy deity,
Never broke vow, from whose eyes never
Flew disdainfull dart
Whose hard heart never,
Slew those rewarders?
Thou art young and fair,
Thy Mother soft and gentle as the air,

Thy holy fire still burning, blown with praier.
Then everlasting Love restrain thy will
'Tis God-like to have power but not to kill.

ANTHONY
This is his Lute: let him have it.

PETER
I grant you; but who strikes it?

ANTHONY
An admirable voice too, hark ye.

PETER
Anthony,
Art sure we are at home?

ANTHONY
Without all doubt, Peter.

PETER
Then this must be the Devil.

ANTHONY
Let it be,

Sing again.
Good Devil sing again: O dainty Devil!
Peter believe it, a most delicate Devil,
The sweetest Devil—

[Enter **FREDERICK** and **DON JOHN**.

FREDERICK
If ye could leave peeping.

DON JOHN
I cannot by no means.

FREDERICK
Then come in softly,
And as ye love your faith, presume no further
Than ye have promised.

DON JOHN
Basta.

FREDERICK

What make you up so early Sir?

DON JOHN
You Sir in your contemplations.

PETER
O pray ye peace Sir.

FREDERICK
Why peace Sir?

PETER
Do you hear?

DON JOHN
'Tis your Lute.

FREDERICK
Pray ye speak softly,
She's playing on't.

ANTHONY
The house is haunted Sir,
For this we have heard this half year.

FREDERICK
Ye saw nothing?

ANTHONY
Not I.

PETER
Nor I Sir.

FREDERICK
Get us our breakfast then,
And make no words on't; we'll undertake this spirit,
If it be one.

ANTHONY
This is no Devil Peter.

Sing.

[Exeunt **SERVANTS**.

Mum, there be Bats abroad.

FREDERICK
Stay, now she sings.

DON JOHN
An Angels voice I'le swear.

FREDERICK
Why did'st thou shrug so?
Either allay this heat; or as I live
I will not trust ye.

DON JOHN
Pass! I warrant ye.

[Exeunt.

[Enter **CONSTANTIA**.

CONSTANTIA
To curse those stars, that men say govern us,
To rail at fortune, fall out with my Fate,
And tax the general world, will help me nothing:
Alas, I am the same still, neither are they
Subject to helps, or hurts: Our own desires
Are our own fates, our own stars, all our fortunes,
Which as we sway 'em, so abuse, or bless us.

[Enter **FREDERICK** and **DON JOHN** peeping.

FREDERICK
Peace to your meditations.

DON JOHN
Pox upon ye,
Stand out o'th' light.

CONSTANTIA
I crave your mercy Sir,
My minde o're-charg'd with care made me unmannerly.

FREDERICK
Pray ye set that mind at rest, all shall be perfect.

DON JOHN
I like the body rare; a handsom body,
A wondrous handsom body: would she would turn:
See, and that spightful puppy be not got
Between me and my light again.

FREDERICK
'Tis done,
As all that you command shall be: the Gentleman
Is safely off all danger.

DON JOHN
O de dios.

CONSTANTIA
How shall I thank ye Sir? how satisfie?

FREDERICK
Speak softly, gentle Lady, all's rewarded,
Now does he melt like Marmalad.

DON JOHN
Nay, 'tis certain,
Thou art the sweetest woman I e're look'd on:
I hope thou art not honest.

FREDERICK
None disturb'd ye?

CONSTANTIA
Not any Sir, nor any sound came near me,
I thank your care.

FREDERICK
'Tis well.

DON JOHN
I would fain pray now,
But the Devil and that flesh there, o' the world,
What are we made to suffer?

FREDERICK
He'll enter;
Pull in your head and be hang'd.

DON JOHN
Hark ye Frederick,
I have brought ye home your Pack-saddle.

FREDERICK
Pox upon ye.

CONSTANTIA

Nay let him enter: fie my Lord the Duke,
Stand peeping at your friends.

FREDERICK
Ye are cozen'd Lady,
Here is no Duke.

CONSTANTIA
I know him full well Signior.

DON JOHN
Hold thee there wench.

FREDERICK
This mad-brain'd fool will spoil all.

CONSTANTIA
I do beseech your grace come in.

DON JOHN
My Grace,
There was a word of comfort.

FREDERICK
Shall he enter?
Who e're he be?

DON JOHN
Well follow'd Frederick.

CONSTANTIA
With all my heart.

FREDERICK
Come in then.

[Enter **DON JOHN**.

DON JOHN
'Bless ye Lady.

FREDERICK
Nay start not, though he be a stranger to ye,
He's of a noble strain, my kinsman, Lady,
My Country-man, and fellow Traveller,
One bed contains us ever, one purse feeds us,
And one faith free between us; do not fear him,
He's truly honest.

DON JOHN
That's a lye.

FREDERICK
And trusty:
Beyond your wishes: valiant to defend,
And modest to converse with, as your blushes.

DON JOHN
Now may I hang my self; this commendation
Has broke the neck of all my hopes: for now
Must I cry, no forsooth, and I forsooth, and surely,
And truly as I live, and as I am honest.
Has done these things for 'nonce too; for he knows
Like a most envious Rascal as he is,
I am not honest, nor desire to be,
Especially this way: h'as watch'd his time,
But I shall quit him.

CONSTANTIA
Sir, I credit ye.

FREDERICK
Go kiss her John.

DON JOHN
Plague o' your commendations.

CONSTANTIA
Sir, I shall now desire to be a trouble.

DON JOHN
Never to me, sweet Lady: Thus I seal
My faith, and all my service.

CONSTANTIA
One word Signior.

DON JOHN
Now 'tis impossible I should be honest,
She kisses with a conjuration
Would make the Devil dance: what points she at?
My leg I warrant, or my well knit body,
Sit fast Don Frederick.

FREDERICK
'Twas given him by that Gentleman

You took such care of; his own being lost i'th' scuffle.

CONSTANTIA
With much joy may he wear it: 'tis a right one,
I can assure ye Gentleman, and right happy
May you be in all fights for that fair service.

FREDERICK
Why do ye blush?

CONSTANTIA
'T had almost cozen'd me,
For not to lye, when I saw that, I look'd for
Another Master of it: but 'tis well.

[Knock within.

FREDERICK
Who's there?

[Enter **ANTHONY**.

Stand ye a little close: Come in Sir,

[Exit **CONSTANTIA**.

Now what's the news with you?

ANTHONY
There is a Gentleman without,
Would speak with Don John.

DON JOHN
Who Sir?

ANTHONY
I do not know Sir, but he shews a man
Of no mean reckoning.

FREDERICK
Let him shew his name,
And then return a little wiser.

ANTHONY
Well Sir.

[Exit **ANTHONY**.

FREDERICK
How do you like her John?

DON JOHN
As well as you Frederick,
For all I am honest: you shall find it so too.

FREDERICK
Art thou not honest?

DON JOHN
Art thou an Ass?
And modest as her blushes? What block-head
Would e're have popt out such a dry Apologie,
For his dear friend? and to a Gentlewoman,
A woman of her youth, and delicacy.
They are arguments to draw them to abhor us.
An honest moral man? 'tis for a Constable:
A handsome man, a wholsome man, a tough man,
A liberal man, a likely man, a man
Made up like Hercules, unslak'd with service:
The same to night, to morrow night, the next night,
And so to perpetuitie of pleasures,
These had been things to hearken to, things catching:
But you have such a spic'd consideration,
Such qualms upon your worships conscience,
Such chil-blains in your bloud, that all things pinch ye,
Which nature, and the liberal world makes custom,
And nothing but fair honour, O sweet honor,
Hang up your Eunuch honour: That I was trusty,
And valiant, were things well put in; but modest!
A modest Gentleman! O wit where wast thou?

FREDERICK
I am sorrie John.

DON JOHN
My Ladies Gentlewoman
Would laugh me to a School-boy, make me blush
With playing with my Codpiece point: fie on thee,
A man of thy discretion?

FREDERICK
It shall be mended:
And henceforth ye shall have your due.

[Enter **ANTHONY**.

DON JOHN
I look for't: How now, who is't?

ANTHONY
A Gentleman of this Town
And calls himself Petruchio.

[Enter **CONSTANTIA**.

DON JOHN
I'le attend him.

CONSTANTIA
How did he call himself?

FREDERICK
Petruchio,
Does it concern you ought?

CONSTANTIA
O Gentlemen,
The hour of my destruction is come on me,
I am discover'd, lost, left to my ruine:
As ever ye had pity—

DON JOHN
Do not fear,
Let the great devil come, he shall come through me:
Lost here, and we about ye?

FREDERICK
Fall before us?

CONSTANTIA
O my unfortunate estate, all angers
Compar'd to his, to his—

FREDERICK
Let his, and all mens,
Whilst we have power and life—stand up for heaven sake.

CONSTANTIA
I have offended heaven too; yet heaven knows—

DON JOHN
We are all evil:
Yet Heaven forbid we should have our deserts.
What is he?

CONSTANTIA
Too too near to my offence Sir;
O he will cut me piece-meal.

FREDERICK
'Tis no Treason?

DON JOHN
Let it be what it will, if he cut here,
I'le find him cut-work.

FREDERICK
He must buy you dear,
With more than common lives.

DON JOHN
Fear not, nor weep not:
By heaven I'le fire the Town before ye perish,
And then, the more the merrier, we'l jog with ye.

FREDERICK
Come in, and dry your eyes.

DON JOHN
Pray no more weeping:
Spoil a sweet face for nothing? my return
Shall end all this I warrant you.

CONSTANTIA
Heaven grant it.

[Exeunt.

SCÆNA TERTIA

Enter **PETRUCHIO**, with a Letter.

PETRUCHIO
This man should be of special rank:
For these commends carry no common way,
No slight worth with 'em:
He shall be he.

[Enter **DON JOHN**.

DON JOHN

'Save ye Sir: I am sorrie
My business was so unmannerly, to make ye
Wait thus long here.

PETRUCHIO

Occasions must be serv'd Sir:
But is your name Don John?

DON JOHN

It is Sir.

PETRUCHIO

Then,
First, for your own brave sake I must embrace ye:
Next, from the credit of your noble friend
Hernando de Alvara, make ye mine:
Who lays his charge upon me in this Letter
To look ye out, and for the goodness in ye,
Whilst your occasions make ye resident
In this place, to supply ye, love and honour ye;
Which had I known sooner—

DON JOHN

Noble Sir,
You'l make my thanks too poor: I wear a sword, Sir,
And have a service to be still dispos'd of,
As you shall please command it.

PETRUCHIO

Gentle Sir,
That manly courtesie is half my business:
And to be short, to make ye know I honour ye,
And in all points believe your worth like Oracle,
And how above my friends, which are not few,
And those not slack, I estimate your vertues,
Make your self understand, This day Petruchio,
A man that may command the strength of this place,
Hazard the boldest spirits, hath made choice
Only of you, and in a noble office.

DON JOHN

Forward, I am free to entertain it.

PETRUCHIO

Thus then:
I do beseech ye mark me.

DON JOHN
I shall do it.

PETRUCHIO
Ferrara's Duke, would I might call him worthie,
But that he has raz'd out from his family,
As he has mine with Infamie, This man,
Rather this powerfull Monster, we being left
But two of all our house, to stock our memories,
My Sister, and my self; with arts, and witchcrafts,
Vows, and such oaths heaven has no mercy for,
Drew to dishonour this weak maid, by stealths,
And secret passages I knew not of,
Oft he obtain'd his wishes, oft abus'd her:
I am asham'd to say the rest: This purchas'd,
And his hot bloud allay'd, as friends forsake us
At a miles end upon our way, he left her,
And all our name to ruine.

DON JOHN
This was foul Play,
And ought to be rewarded so.

PETRUCHIO
I hope so;
He scap'd me yester-night: which if he dare
Again adventure for, Heaven pardon him,
I shall with all my heart.

DON JOHN
For me, brave Signior,
What do ye intend?

PETRUCHIO
Only, fair Sir, this trust,
Which from the commendations of this Letter,
I dare presume well plac'd, nobly to bear him
By word of mouth a single challenge from me,
That man to man, if he have honour in him,
We may decide all difference.

DON JOHN
Fair, and noble,
And I will do it home: When shall I visite ye?

PETRUCHIO
Please you this after-noon, I will ride with you:
For at a Castle six miles hence, we are sure

To find him.

DON JOHN
I'le be ready.

PETRUCHIO
To attend ye,
My man shall wait: with all my love.

[Exit **PETRUCHIO**.

DON JOHN
My service shall not fail ye.

[Enter **FREDERICK**.

FREDERICK
How now?

DON JOHN
All's well: who dost thou think this wench is?
Ghess, and thou canst?

FREDERICK
I cannot.

DON JOHN
Be it known then,
To all men by these presents, this is she,
She, she, and only she, our curious coxcombs
Were errant two moneths after.

FREDERICK
Who, Constantia?
Thou talk'st of Cocks and Bulls.

DON JOHN
I talk of wenches,
Of cocks and Hens Don Frederick; this is the Pullet
We two went proud after.

FREDERICK
It cannot be.

DON JOHN
It shall be;
Sister to Don Petruchio: I know all man.

FREDERICK
Now I believe.

DON JOHN
Go to, there has been stirring,
Fumbling with Linnen Frederick.

FREDERICK
'Tis impossible,
You know her fame was pure as fire.

DON JOHN
That pure fire
Has melted out her maiden-head: she is crackt:
We have all that hope of our side, boy.

FREDERICK
Thou tell'st me,
To my imagination, things incredible:
I see no loose thought in her.

DON JOHN
That's all one,
She is loose i'th' hilts by heaven: but the world must know
A fair way, upon vow of marriage.

FREDERICK
There may be such a slip.

DON JOHN
And will be, Frederick,
Whil'st the old game's a foot: I fear the boy
Will prove hers too I took up.

FREDERICK
Good circumstance
May cure all this yet.

DON JOHN
There thou hitst it, Frederick:
Come, let's walk in and comfort her: her being here
Is nothing yet suspected: anon I'le tell thee
Wherefore her Brother came, who by this light
Is a brave noble fellow, and what honour
H'as done to me a stranger: there be Irons
Heating for some, will hiss into their heart blouds,
E're all be ended; so much for this time.

FREDERICK
Well Sir.

[Exeunt.

Enter **LANDLADY** and **PETER**.

LANDLADY
Come, ye do know.

PETER
I do not by this hand Mistris.
But I suspect.

LANDLADY
What?

PETER
That if egges continue
At this price, women will ne're be sav'd
By their good works.

LANDLADY
I will know.

PETER
Ye shall, any thing
Lyes in my power: The Duke of Loraine now
Is seven thousand strong: I heard it of a fish-wife,
A woman of fine knowledge.

LANDLADY
Sirrah, Sirrah.

PETER
The Popes Bulls are broke loose too, and 'tis suspected
They shall be baited in England.

LANDLADY
Very well Sir.

PETER

No, 'tis not so well neither.

LANDLADY
But I say to ye,
Who is it keeps your Master company?

PETER
I say to you, Don John.

LANDLADY
I say what woman?

PETER
I say so too.

LANDLADY
I say again, I will know.

PETER
I say 'tis fit ye should.

LANDLADY
And I tell thee
He has a woman here.

PETER
And I tell thee
'Tis then the better for him.

LANDLADY
You are no Bawd now?

PETER
Would I were able to be call'd unto it:
A worshipfull vocation for my elders;
For as I understand it is a place
Fitting my betters far.

LANDLADY
Was ever Gentlewoman
So frumpt off with a fool? well sawcy Sirrah,
I will know who it is, and for what purpose;
I pay the rent, and I will know how my house
Comes by these Inflammations: if this geer hold,
Best hang a sign-post up, to tell the Signiors,
Here ye may have lewdness at Liverie.

[Enter **FREDERICK**.

PETER
'Twould be a great ease to your age.

FREDERICK
How now?
Why what's the matter Land-lady?

LANDLADY
What's the matter?
Ye use me decently among ye Gentlemen.

FREDERICK
Who has abus'd her, you Sir?

LANDLADY
'Ods my witness
I will not be thus treated, that I will not.

PETER
I gave her no ill language.

LANDLADY
Thou lyest lewdly,
Thou tookst me up at every word I spoke,
As I had been a Mawkin, a flurt Gillian;
And thou thinkst, because thou canst write and read,
Our noses must be under thee.

FREDERICK
Dare you Sirrah?

PETER
Let but the truth be known Sir, I beseech ye,
She raves of wenches, and I know not what Sir.

LANDLADY
Go to, thou know'st too well, thou wicked varlet,
Thou instrument of evil.

PETER
As I live Sir,
She is ever thus till dinner.

FREDERICK
Get ye in,
I'le answer you anon Sir.

PETER
By this hand
I'le break your Posset pan.

[Exit.

LANDLADY
Then by this hood
I'le lock the meat up.

FREDERICK
Now your grief, what is't?
For I can ghesse—

LANDLADY
Ye may with shame enough,
If there were shame amongst ye; nothing thought on,
But how ye may abuse my house? not satisfi'd
With bringing home your Bastards to undoe me,
But you must drill your whores here too? my patience
(Because I bear, and bear, and carry all,
And as they say am willing to groan under)
Must be your make-sport now.

FREDERICK
No more of these words,
Nor no more murmurings Lady: for you know
That I know something. I did suspect your anger,
But turn it presently and handsomely,
And bear your self discreetly to this woman,
For such an one there is indeed.

LANDLADY
'Tis well son.

FREDERICK
Leaving your devils Matins, and your melancholies,
Or we shall leave our lodgings.

LANDLADY
You have much need
To use these vagrant ways, and to much profit:
Ye had that might content
(At home within your selves too) right good Gentlemen,
Wholsome, and ye said handsom: But you gallants,
Beast that I was to believe ye—

FREDERICK

Leave your suspicion:
For as I live there's no such thing.

LANDLADY
Mine honour;
And 'twere not for mine honour.

FREDERICK
Come, your honour,
Your house, and you too, if you dare believe me,
Are well enough: sleek up your self, leave crying,
For I must have ye entertain this Lady
With all civility, she well deserves it,
Together with all secresie: I dare trust ye,
For I have found ye faithfull: when you know her,
You will find your own fault: no more words, but do it.

LANDLADY
You know you may command me.

[Enter **DON JOHN**.

DON JOHN
Worshipful Lady,
How does thy velvet Scabbard? by this hand
Thou lookst most amiably, now could I willingly,
And 'twere not for abusing thy Geneva print there,
Venture my Body with thee.

LANDLADY
You'll leave this Roguery
When you come to my years.

DON JOHN
By this light
Thou art not above fifteen yet, a meer Girl,
Thou hast not half thy teeth: come—

FREDERICK
Prithee John
Let her alone, she has been vex'd already;
She'll grow stark mad, man.

DON JOHN
I would see her mad,
An old mad woman—

FREDERICK

Prithee be patient.

DON JOHN
Is like a Millers Mare, troubled with tooth-ach.
She'll make the rarest faces.

FREDERICK
Go, and do it,
And do not mind this fellow.

LANDLADY
Well, Don John,
There will be times again; when O good Mother,
What's good for a Carnosity in the Bladder?
O the green water, Mother.

DON JOHN
Doting take ye;
Do ye remember that?

FREDERICK
She has paid ye now, Sir.

LANDLADY
Clary, sweet mother, clary.

FREDERICK
Are ye satisfied?

LANDLADY
I'll never whore again, never give petticoats
And Wastcoats at five pound apiece: good mother,
Quickly mother; now mock on Son.

DON JOHN
A Devil grind your old Chaps.

[Exit **LANDLADY**.

FREDERICK
By this hand, wench,
I'll give thee a new hood for this.
Has she met with your Lordship?

DON JOHN
Touch-wood take her.

[Enter **ANTHONY**.

She's a rare ghostly Mother.

ANTHONY
Below attends ye
The Gentlemans man, Sir, that was with you.

DON JOHN
Well, Sir;
My time is come then; yet if my project hold,
You shall not stay behind; I'll rather trust

[Enter **CONSTANTIA**.

A Cat with sweet milk, Frederick; by her face,
I feel her fears are working.

CONSTANTIA
Is there no way,
I do beseech ye think yet, to divert
This certain danger?

FREDERICK
'Tis impossible;
Their Honours are engag'd.

CONSTANTIA
Then there must be murther,
Which, Gentlemen, I shall no sooner hear of,
Than make one in't: you may if you please, Sir,
Make all go less yet.

DON JOHN
Lady, were't mine own Cause,
I could dispense; but loaden with my friends trust,
I must go on; though general massacres
As much I fear—

CONSTANTIA
Do ye hear, Sir; for Heavens pity
Let me request one love of you.

FREDERICK
Yes, any thing.

CONSTANTIA
This Gentleman I find too resolute,
Too hot and fiery for the Cause; as ever

You did a vertuous deed, for honours sake
Go with him, and allay him; your fair temper
And noble disposition, like wish'd showrs,
May quench those eating fires, that would spoil all else.
I see in him destruction.

FREDERICK
I will do it;
And 'tis a wise consideration,
To me a bounteous favour, hark ye, John;
I will go with ye.

DON JOHN
No.

FREDERICK
Indeed I will,
Ye go upon a hazard; no denial,
For as I live, I'll go.

DON JOHN
Then make ye ready,
For I am straight o' horse-back.

FREDERICK
My Sword on,
I am as ready as you; what my best labour,
With all the art I have can work upon 'em,
Be sure of, and expect fair end; the old Gentlewoman
Shall wait upon you; she is both grave and private,
And ye may trust her in all points.

CONSTANTIA
You are noble;
And so I kiss your hand.

DON JOHN
That seal for me too,
And I hope happy issue, Lady.

CONSTANTIA
All Heavens Care upon ye, and my Prayers.

DON JOHN
So,
Now my mind's at rest.

FREDERICK

Away, 'tis late, Don John

[Exeunt.

Enter **ANTONIO**, a **SURGEON**, and **TWO GENTLEMEN**.

FIRST GENTLEMEN
Come, Sir, be hearty, all the worst is past.

ANTONIO
Give me some Wine.

SURGEON
'Tis death, Sir.

ANTONIO
'Tis a Horse, Sir.
To be drest to the tune of Ale only!
Nothing but sawces to my sores!

SECOND GENTLEMEN
Fie, Antonio,
You must be govern'd.

ANTONIO
H'as given me a damn'd Clyster,
Only of sand and snow water, Gentlemen,
Has almost scour'd my guts out.

SURGEON
I have giv'n you that, Sir,
Is fittest for your state.

ANTONIO
And here he feeds me
With rotten ends of Rooks, and drown'd Chickens,
Stew'd Pericraniums, and Pia-maters;
And when I go to bed (by Heaven 'tis true Gentlemen)
He rolls me up in Lints, with Labels at 'em,
That I am just the man i'th' Almanack,
In Head and Face, is Aries place.

SURGEON
Will't please ye

To let your friends see you open'd?

ANTONIO
Will't please you, Sir,
To let me have a wench? I feel my Body
Open enough for that yet.

SURGEON
How, a Wench?

ANTONIO
Why look ye, Gentlemen; thus I am us'd still,
I can get nothing that I want.

FIRST GENTLEMEN
Leave these things,
And let him open ye.

ANTONIO
D'ye hear, Surgeon?
Send for the Musick, let me have some pleasure
To entertain my friends, besides your Sallads,
Your green salves, and your searches, and some Wine too,
That I may only smell to it; or by this light
I'll dye upon thy hand, and spoil thy custome.

FIRST GENTLEMEN
Let him have Musick.

[Enter **ROWLAND** with Wine.

SURGEON
'Tis in the house, and ready,
If he will ask no more but Wine—

[Musick.

SECOND GENTLEMEN
He shall not drink it.

SURGEON
Will these things please ye?

ANTHONY
Yes, and let 'em sing
John Dorrie.

SECOND GENTLEMEN

'Tis too long.

ANTHONY
I'll have John Dorrie,
For to that warlike tune I will be open'd:
Give me some drink, have ye stopt the leaks well, Surgeon,
All will run out else?

SURGEON
Fear not.

ANTHONY
Sit down, Gentlemen:
And now advance your Plaisters.

[Song of John Dorrie.

Give 'em ten shillings, friends; how do ye find me?
What symptoms do you see now?

SURGEON
None, Sir, dangerous;
But if you will be rul'd—

ANTHONY
What time?

SURGEON
I can cure you
In forty days, if you will not transgress me.

ANTHONY
I have a Dog shall lick me whole in twenty;
In how long canst thou kill me?

SURGEON
Presently.

ANTHONY
Do it, there's more delight in't.

FIRST GENTLEMEN
You must have patience.

ANTHONY
Man, I must have business; this foolish fellow
Hinders himself; I have a dozen Rascals
To hurt within these five days; good man-mender,

Stop me with some Parsley, like stuft Beef,
And let me walk abroad.

SURGEON
Ye shall walk shortly.

ANTHONY
For I must find Petruchio.

SECOND GENTLEMEN
Time enough.

FIRST GENTLEMEN
Come, lead him in, and let him sleep: within these three days
We'll beg ye leave to play.

SECOND GENTLEMEN
And then how things fall,
We'll certainly inform ye.

ANTHONY
But Surgeon, promise me
I shall drink Wine then too.

SURGEON
A little temper'd.

ANTHONY
Nay, I'll no tempering, Surgeon.

SURGEON
Well, as't please ye,
So ye exceed not.

ANTHONY
Farewell: and if ye find
The mad Slave that thus slash'd me, commend me to him,
And bid him keep his Skin close.

FIRST GENTLEMEN
Take your rest, Sir.

[Exeunt.

SCÆNA TERTIA

Enter **CONSTANTIA**, and **LANDLADY**.

CONSTANTIA
I have told ye all I can, and more than yet
Those Gentlemen know of me; ever trusting
Your Counsel and Concealment; for to me
You seem a worthy Woman; one of those
Are seldome found in our Sex, wise and vertuous,
Direct me I beseech ye.

LANDLADY
Ye say well, Lady,
And hold ye to that point, for in these businesses
A Womans Counsel that conceives the matter,
(Do ye mark me? that conceives the matter, Lady)
Is worth ten mens engagements: She knows something,
And out of that can work like Wax; when men
Are giddy-headed, either out of Wine,
Or a more Drunkenness, vain Ostentation,
Discovering all; there is no more keep in 'em
Than hold upon an Eeles tail; Nay, 'tis held fashion
To defame now all they can.

CONSTANTIA
I, but these Gentlemen—

LANDLADY
Do not you trust to that; these Gentlemen
Are as all Gentlemen of the same Barrel;
I, and the self same pickle too. Be it granted,
They have us'd ye with respect and fair behaviour,
Ere since ye came, do you know what must follow?
They are Spaniards, Lady, Gennets of high mettle,
Things that will thrash the Devil, or his Dam,
Let 'em appear but cloven.

CONSTANTIA
Now Heaven bless me.

LANDLADY
Mad Colts will court the wind; I know 'em, Lady,
To the least hair they have; and I tell you,
Old as I am, let but the pint pot bless 'em,
They'll offer to my years—

CONSTANTIA
How?

LANDLADY
Such rude gambols—

CONSTANTIA
To you?

LANDLADY
I, and so handle me, that oft I am forc'd
To fight of all four for my safety; there's the younger,
Don John, the arrantest Jack in all this City;
The other, Time has blasted, yet he will stoop,
If not o'rflown, and freely on the quarry;
Has been a Dragon in his days. But Tarmont,
Don Jenkin is the Devil himself, the dog-days,
The most incomprehensible Whore-master,
Twenty a night is nothing; Beggars, Broom-women,
And those so miserable, they look like famine,
Are all sweet Ladies in his drink.

CONSTANTIA
He's a handsome Gentleman;
Pity he should be master of such follies.

LANDLADY
He's ne'r without a noise of Sirynges
In's Pocket, those proclaim him; birding Pills,
Waters to cool his Conscience, in small Viols:
With thousand such sufficient emblems; the truth is,
Whose Chastity he chops upon he cares not,
He flies at all; Bastards upon my conscience,
He has now in making, multitudes; the last night
He brought home one; I pity her that bore it,
But we are all weak Vessels, some rich Woman
(For wise I dare not call her) was the mother,
For it was hung with Jewels; the bearing Cloath
No less than Crimson Velvet.

CONSTANTIA
How?

LANDLADY
'Tis true, Lady.

CONSTANTIA
Was it a Boy too?

LANDLADY
A brave Boy; deliberation

And judgment shew'd in's getting, as I'll say for him,
He's as well paced for that sport—

CONSTANTIA
May I see it?
For there is a neighbour of mine, a Gentlewoman,
Has had a late mischance, which willingly
I would know further of; now if you please
To be so courteous to me.

LANDLADY
Ye shall see it:
But what do ye think of these men now ye know 'em,
And of the cause I told ye of? Be wise,
Ye may repent too late else; I but tell you
For your own good, and as you will find it, Lady.

CONSTANTIA
I am advis'd.

LANDLADY
No more words then; do that,
And instantly, I told ye of, be ready;
Don John, I'll fit you for your frumps.

CONSTANTIA
I shall be:
But shall I see this Child?

LANDLADY
Within this half hour,
Let's in, and there think better; she that's wise,
Leaps at occasion first; the rest pay for it.

[Exeunt.

SCÆNA QUARTA

Enter **PETRUCHIO, DON JOHN**, and **FREDERICK**.

DON JOHN
Sir, he is worth your knowledge, and a Gentleman
If I that so much love him, may commend him,
Of free and vertuous parts; and one, if foul play
Should fall upon us, for which fear I brought him,
Will not flye back for phillips.

PETER
Ye much honour me,
And once more I pronounce ye both mine.

FREDERICK
Stay, what Troop
Is that below i' th' Valley there?

DON JOHN
Hawking I take it.

PETER
They are so; 'tis the Duke, 'tis even he, Gentlemen,
Sirrah, draw back the Horses till we call ye,
I know him by his Company.

FREDERICK
I think too
He bends up this way.

PETER
So he does.

DON JOHN
Stand you still
Within that Covert till I call: you, Frederick,
By no means be not seen, unless they offer
To bring on odds upon us; he comes forward,
Here will I wait him fairly: to your Cabins.

PETER
I need no more instruct ye?

DON JOHN
Fear me not,
I'le give it him, and boldly.

[Exit **PETER** and **FREDERICK**.

[Enter **DUKE** and his **FACTION**.

DUKE
Feed the Hawks up,
We'll flie no more to day, O my blest fortune!
Have I so fairly met the man?

DON JOHN

Ye have, Sir,
And him you know by this.

DUKE
Sir all the honour,
And love—

DON JOHN
I do beseech your Grace stay there,
(For I know you too now) that love and honour
I come not to receive; nor can you give it,
Till ye appear fair to the world; I must beseech ye
Dismiss your train a little.

DUKE
Walk aside,
And out of hearing I command ye: Now, Sir.

DON JOHN
Last time we met, I was a friend.

DUKE
And Nobly,
You did a friends office: let your business
Be what it may, you must be still—

DON JOHN
Your pardon,
Never a friend to him, cannot be friend
To his own honour.

DUKE
In what have I transgress'd it?
Ye make a bold breach at the first, Sir.

DON JOHN
Bolder,
You made that breach that let in infamy,
And ruine, to surprise a noble stock.

DUKE
Be plain, Sir.

DON JOHN
I will, and short;
Ye have wrong'd a Gentleman,
Little behind your self, beyond all justice,
Beyond mediation of all friends.

DUKE
The man, and manner of wrong?

DON JOHN
Petruchio,
The wrong, ye have Whor'd his Sister.

DUKE
What's his will in't?

DON JOHN
His will is to oppose you like a Gentleman,
And single, to decide all.

DUKE
Now stay you, Sir,
And hear me with the like belief: this Gentleman,
His Sister that you nam'd, 'tis true I have long lov'd,
Nor was that love lascivious, as he makes it;
As true, I have enjoy'd her: no less truth,
I have a Child by her: but that she, or he,
Or any of that family are tainted,
Suffer disgrace, or ruin, by my pleasures,
I wear a Sword to satisfie the world no,
And him in this cause when he please; for know, Sir,
She is my Wife, contracted before Heaven,
(Witness I owe more tye to, than her Brother)
Nor will I flye from that name, which long since
Had had the Churches approbation,
But for his jealous danger.

DON JOHN
Sir, your pardon,
And all that was my anger, now my service.

DUKE
Fair Sir, I knew I should convert ye; had we
But that rough man here now too—

DON JOHN
And ye shall, Sir,
Whoa, hoa, hoo.

DUKE
I hope ye have laid no Ambush?

[Enter **PETRUCHIO**.

DON JOHN
Only friends.

DUKE
My noble Brother welcome:
Come put your anger off, we'll no fighting,
Unless you will maintain I am unworthy
To bear that name.

PETER
Do you speak this heartily?

DUKE
Upon my soul, and truly; the first Priest
Shall put you out of these doubts.

PETER
Now I love ye;
And I beseech you pardon my suspicions,
You are now more than a Brother, a brave friend too.

DON JOHN
The good man's over-joy'd.

[Enter **FREDERICK**.

FREDERICK
How, how, how goes it?

DON JOHN
Why, the man has his Mare again, and all's well, Frederick,
The Duke professes freely he's her Husband.

FREDERICK
'Tis a good hearing.

DON JOHN
Yes, for modest Gentlemen.
I must present ye: may it please your Grace,
To number this brave Gentleman, my friend,
And noble kinsman, amongst those your servants.

DUKE
O my brave friend! you shower your bounties on me
Amongst my best thoughts, Signior, in which number
You being worthily dispos'd already,
May place your friend to honour me.

FREDERICK
My love, Sir,
And where your Grace dares trust me, all my service.

PETER
Why! this is wondrous happy: But now Brother,
Now comes the bitter to our sweet: Constantia.

DUKE
Why, what of her?

PETER
Nor what, nor where, do I know!
Wing'd with her fears last night, beyond my knowledge,
She quit my house, but whither—

FREDERICK
Let not that—

DUKE
No more good Sir, I have heard too much.

PETER
Nay sink not,
She cannot be so lost.

DON JOHN
Nor shall not, Gentlemen;
Be free again, the Lady's found; that smile, Sir,
Shews ye distrust your Servant.

DUKE
I do beseech ye.

DON JOHN
Ye shall believe me: by my soul she is safe.

DUKE
Heaven knows, I would believe, Sir.

FREDERICK
Ye may safely.

DON JOHN
And under noble usage: this fair Gentleman
Met her in all her doubts last night, and to his Guard,
(Her fears being strong upon her) she gave her person,

Who waited on her to our lodging; where all respect,
Civil and honest service now attend her.

PETER
Ye may believe now.

DUKE
Yes, I do, and strongly:
Well my good friends, or rather my good Angels,
For ye have both preserv'd me; when these vertues
Dye in your friends remembrance—

DON JOHN
Good your Grace,
Lose no more time in complement, 'tis too precious,
I know it by my self there can be no Hell
To his that hangs upon his hopes; especially
In way of lustly pleasures.

PETER
He has hit it.

FREDERICK
To horse again then, for this night I'le crown
With all the joyes ye wish for.

PETER
Happy Gentlemen.

[Exeunt.

[Enter **FRANCISCO**.

FRANCISCO
This is the maddest mischief: never fool
Was so fob'd off, as I am; made ridiculous,
And to my self mine own Ass: trust a Woman?
I'le trust the Devil first; for he dare be
Better than's word sometime: what faith have I broke?
In what observance fail'd? Let me consider,

[Enter **DON JOHN** and **FREDERICK**.

For this is monstrous usage.

FREDERICK
Let them talk,
We'll ride on fair and softly.

FRANCISCO
Well, Constantia.

FREDERICK
Constantia, what's this fellow? stay by all means.

FRANCISCO
Ye have spun your self a fair thread now.

FREDERICK
Stand still, John.

FRANCISCO
What cause had you to fly? what fear possest ye?
Were you not safely lodg'd from all suspicion?
Us'd with all gentle means? did any know
How ye came thither, or what your sin was.

FREDERICK
John,
I smell some juggling, John.

DON JOHN
Yes, Frederick, I fear it will be found so.

FRANCISCO
So strangely,
Without the counsel of your friends; so desperately
To put all dangers on ye?

FREDERICK
'Tis she.

FRANCISCO
So deceitfully,
After a strangers lure!

DON JOHN
Did ye mark that, Frederick?

FRANCISCO
To make ye appear more monster; and the Law
More cruel to reward ye? to leave all,
All that should be your safegard, to seek evils?
Was this your wisdom? this your promise? well,
He that incited ye—

FREDERICK
Mark that too.

DON JOHN
Yes Sir.

FRANCISCO
'Had better have plough'd farther off; now Lady,
What will your last friend, he that should preserve ye,
And hold your credit up, the brave Antonio,
Think of this slip? he'll to Petruchio,
And call for open justice.

DON JOHN
'Tis she, Frederick.

FREDERICK
But what that he is, John?

FRANCISCO
I do not doubt yet
To bolt ye out, for I know certainly
Ye are about the Town still: ha, no more words.

[Exit.

FREDERICK
Well.

DON JOHN
Very well.

FREDERICK
Discreetly.

DON JOHN
Finely carried.

FREDERICK
You have no more of these tricks?

DON JOHN
Ten to one, Sir,
I shall meet with 'em if ye have.

FREDERICK
Is this honest?

DON JOHN
Was it in you a friends part to deal double?
I am no Ass Don Frederick.

FREDERICK
And Don John,
It shall appear I am no fool;
Disgrace me to make your self a lecher?
'Tis boyish, 'tis base.

DON JOHN
'Tis false, and most unmanly to upbraid me,
Nor will I be your bolster, Sir.

FREDERICK
Thou wanton boy, thou hadst better have been Eunuch,
Thou common womans courtesie, than thus
Lascivious, basely to have bent mine honour.
A friend? I'le make a horse my friend first.

DON JOHN
Holla, holla,
Ye kick too fast, Sir: what strange brains have you got,
That dare crow out thus bravely? I better been an Eunuch?
I privy to this dog trick? clear your self,
For I know where the wind sits, and most nobly,
Or as I have a life—

FREDERICK
No more: they're horses.

[A noise within like horses.

Nor shew no discontent: to morrow comes;
Let's quietly away: if she be at home,
Our jealousies are put off.

DON JOHN
The fellow,

[Enter **DUKE**, **PETRUCHIO**.

We have lost him in our spleens, like fools.

DUKE
Come, Gentlemen,
Now set on roundly: suppose ye have all Mistresses,
And mend your pace according.

PETRUCHIO
Then have at ye.

[Exeunt.

Enter **DUKE**, **PETRUCHIO**, **FREDERICK**, and **DON JOHN**.

PETRUCHIO
Now to Bologna, my most honoured Brother,
I dare pronounce ye a hearty, and safe welcome,
Our loves shall now way-lay ye; welcome, Gentlemen.

DON JOHN
The same to you brave Sir; Don Frederick,
Will ye step in and give the Lady notice
Who comes to honour her?

PETRUCHIO
Bid her be sudden,
We come to see no curious wench: a night-gown
Will serve the turn: here's one that knows her nearer.

FREDERICK
I'le tell her what ye say, Sir.

[Exit **FREDERICK**.

DUKE
My dear brother,
Ye are a merry Gentleman.

PETRUCHIO
Now will the sport be,
To observe her alterations; how like a wildfire
She'll leap into your bosom; then seeing me,
Her conscience, and her fears creeping upon her,
Dead as a fowl at souse, she'll sink.

DUKE
Fair Brother,
I must intreat you—

PETRUCHIO
I conceive your mind, Sir,
I will not chide her: yet ten Duckets, Duke,
She falls upon her knees, ten more she dare not—

DUKE
I must not have her frighted.

PETRUCHIO
Well you shall not:

[Enter **FREDERICK** and **PETER**.

But like a Summers evening against heat,
Mark how I'le guild her cheeks!

DON JOHN
How now?

FREDERICK
Ye may, Sir:
Not to abuse your patience, noble friends,
Nor hold ye off with tedious circumstance,
For you must know—

PETRUCHIO
What?

DUKE
Where is she?

FREDERICK
Gone, Sir.

DUKE
How?

PETRUCHIO
What did you say, Sir?

FREDERICK
Gone, by Heaven removed,
The woman of the house too.

DON JOHN
Well Don Frederick.

FREDERICK
Don John, it is not well, but—

PETER
Gone?

FREDERICK
This fellow
Can testifie I lye not.

PETER
Some four hours after
My Master was departed, with this Gentleman,
My fellow and my self being sent of business,
(As we must think) of purpose—

PETRUCHIO
Hang these circumstances,
They appear like Owls, to ill ends.

DON JOHN
Now could I eat
The Devil in his own broth, I am so tortur'd.
Gone?

PETRUCHIO
Gone?

FREDERICK
Directly gone, fled, shifted: what would you have me say?

DUKE
Well, Gentlemen,
Wrong not my good opinion.

FREDERICK
For your Dukedom
I will not be a Knave, Sir.

DON JOHN
He that is,
A rot run in his bloud.

PETRUCHIO
But hark ye Gentlemen,
Are ye sure ye had her here, did ye not dream this?

DON JOHN

Have you your nose, Sir?

PETRUCHIO
Yes, Sir.

DON JOHN
Then we had her.

PETRUCHIO
Since you are so short, believe your having her
Shall suffer more construction.

DON JOHN
Let it suffer,
But if I be not clear of all dishonour,
Or practice that may taint my reputation,
And ignorant of where this Woman is,
Make me your Cities monster.

DUKE
I believe ye.

DON JOHN
I could lye with a Witch now, to be reveng'd,
Upon that Rascal did this.

FREDERICK
Only thus much
I would desire your Grace, for my mind gives me
Before night yet she is yours: stop all opinion,
And let no anger out, till full cause call it,
Then every mans own work's to justifie him,
And this day let us give to search: my man here
Tells me, by chance he saw out of a window
(Which place he has taken notice of) such a face
As our old Landladies, he believes the same too,
And by her hood assures it: Let's first thither,
For she being found, all's ended.

DUKE
Come, for Heavens sake,
And Fortune, and thou be'st not ever turning,
If there be one firm step in all thy reelings,
Now settle it, and save my hopes: away friends.

[Exeunt.

Enter **ANTONIO** and his **SERVANT**.

ANTONIO
With all my Jewels?

SERVANT
All, Sir.

ANTONIO
And that mony
I left i'th' trunk?

SERVANT
The Trunk broke, and that gone too.

ANTONIO
Francisco of the plot?

SERVANT
Gone with the wench too.

ANTONIO
The mighty pox go with 'em: belike they thought
I was no man of this world, and those trifles
Would but disturb my conscience.

SERVANT
Sure they thought, Sir,
You would not live to persecute 'em.

ANTONIO
Whore and Fidler,
Why, what a consort have they made! Hen and Bacon!
Well my sweet Mistris, well good Madam mar-tail?
You that have hung about my neck, and lick't me,
I'le try how handsomely your Ladyship
Can hang upon a Gallows, there's your Master-piece;
But hark ye Sirrah, no imagination
Of where they should be?

SERVANT
None, Sir, yet we have search'd
All places we suspected; I believe, Sir,
They have taken towards the Ports.

ANTONIO
Get me a conjurer,
One that can raise a water Devil, I'le port 'em;
Play at duck and drake with my mony; take heed Fidler;
I'le dance ye by this hand, your Fidle-stick
I'le grease of a new fashion, for presuming
To meddle with my degamboys: get me a Conjurer,
Enquire me out a man that lets out Devils:
None but my C. Cliffe serve your turn?

SERVANT
I know not—

ANTONIO
In every street, Tom fool, any blear-ey'd people
With red heads, and flat noses can perform it;
Thou shalt know 'em by their half Gowns and no Breeches:
Mount my Mare Fidler? ha boy! up at first dash?
Sit sure, I'le clap a nettle, and a smart one,
Shall make your Filly firk: I will fine Fidler,
I'le put you to your plunge, Boy: Sirrah meet me
Some two hours hence at home; in the mean time
Find out a conjurer and know his price,
How he will let his Devils by the day out,
I'le have 'em, and they be above ground.

[Exit **ANTONIO**.

SERVANT
Now bless me,
What a mad man is this! I must do something
To please his humour: such a man I'le ask for,
And tell him where he is: but to come near him,
Or have any thing to do with his don Devils,
I thank my fear, I dare not, nor I will not.

[Exit.

SCÆNA TERTIA

Enter **DUKE, PETRUCHIO, FREDERICK, DON JOHN, PETER** and **SERVANT** with Bottle.

FREDERICK
Whither wilt thou lead us?

PETRUCHIO

'Tis hard by, Sir.
And ten to one this wine goes thither.

DUKE
Forward.

PETRUCHIO
Are they grown so merry?

DUKE
'Tis most likely,
She has heard of this good fortune, and determines
To wash her sorrows off.

PETRUCHIO
'Tis so; that house, Sir,
Is it: out of that window certainly
I saw my old Mistresses face.

PETRUCHIO
They are merry indeed,

[Musick.

Hark I hear Musick too.

DUKE
Excellent Musick.

DON JOHN
Would I were ev'n among 'em, and alone now;
A pallat for the purpose in a corner,
And good rich Wine within me; what gay sport
Could I make in an hour now!

SONG.
Welcome sweet liberty, and care farewel,
I am mine own,
She is twice damn'd, that lives in Hell,
When Heaven is shown.
Budding beauty, blooming years
Were made for pleasure, farewel fears,
For now I am my self, mine own command,
My fortune alwayes in my hand.

FREDERICK
Hark a voice too;
Let's not stir yet by any means.

DON JOHN
Was this her own voice?

DUKE
Yes, sure.

FREDERICK
'Tis a rare one.

[Enter **BAWD**, above.

DUKE
The Song confirms her here too: for if ye mark it,
It spake of liberty, and free enjoying
The happy end of pleasure.

PETRUCHIO
Look ye there, Sir,
Do ye know that head?

FREDERICK
'Tis my good Landlady,
I find fear has done all this.

DON JOHN
She I swear,
And now do I know by the hanging of her Hood,
She is parcel drunk: shall we go in?

DUKE
Not yet, Sir.

PETRUCHIO
No, let 'em take their pleasure.

DUKE
When it is highest,

[Musick.

We'll step in, and amaze 'em: peace, more Musick.

DON JOHN
This Musick murders me: what bloud have I now!

FREDERICK
I should know that face.

[Enter **FRANCISCO** and Exit.

DON JOHN
By this light 'tis he, Frederick,
That bred our first suspicions, the same fellow.

FREDERICK
He that we overtook, and overheard too,
Discoursing of Constantia.

DON JOHN
Still the same;
Now he slips in.

DUKE
What's that?

FREDERICK
She must be here Sir:
This is the very fellow, I told your Grace

[Enter **FRANCISCO**.

We found upon the way; and what his talk was.

PETRUCHIO
Why, sure I know this fellow; yes, 'tis he,
Francisco, Antonio's boy, a rare Musician,
He taught my Sister on the Lute, and is ever
(She loves his voice so well) about her: certain,
Without all doubt she is here: it must be so.

DON JOHN
Here? that's no question: what should our hen
Do here without her? if she be not here (o'th' game else
I am so confident) let your grace believe,
We two are arrant Rascals, and have abus'd ye.

FREDERICK
I say so too.

DON JOHN
Why there's the hood again now,
The guard that guides us; I know the fabrick of it,
And know the old tree of that saddle yet, 'twas made of,
A hunting hood, observe it.

DUKE
Who shall enter?

PETRUCHIO
I'le make one.

DON JOHN
I, another.

DUKE
But so carry it,
That all her joyes flow not together.

DON JOHN
If we told her,
Your grace would none of her?

DUKE
By no means Signior,
'Twould turn her wild, stark frantick.

DON JOHN
Or assur'd her—

DUKE
Nothing of that stern nature: this ye may Sir,
That the conditions of our fear yet stand
On nice and dangerous knittings: or that a little
I seem to doubt the child.

DON JOHN
Would I could draw her
To hate your grace with these things.

PETRUCHIO
Come let's enter.

[Exit **PETRUCHIO** and **DON JOHN**.

And now he sees me not, I'le search her soundly.

DUKE
Now luck of all sides.

[Musick.

FREDERICK
Doubt it not: more Musick:

Sure she has heard some comfort.

DUKE
Yes, stand still Sir.

FREDERICK
This is the maddest song.

DUKE
Applyed for certain
To some strange melancholy she is loaden with.

FREDERICK
Now all the sport begins—hark!

DUKE
They are amongst 'em,
The fears now, and the shakings!

[Trampling above.

FREDERICK
Our old Lady
(Hark how they run) is even now at this instant
Ready to lose her head-piece by Don John,
Or creeping through a Cat hole.

[**PETRUCHIO** and **DON JOHN** within.

PETRUCHIO
Bring 'em down,
And you Sir, follow me.

DUKE
He's angry with 'em,
I must not suffer this.

DON JOHN [within]
Bowl down the Bawd there
Old Erra mater: you Lady leachery,
For the good will I bear to th' game, most tenderly
Shall be lead out, and lash'd.

[Enter **PETRUCHIO**, **DON JOHN**, **WHORE**, and **BAWD** with **FRANCISCO**.

DUKE
Is this Constantia?
Why Gentlemen? what do you mean? is this she?

WHORE
I am Constantia Sir.

DUKE
A whore ye are Sir.

WHORE
'Tis very true: I am a whore indeed Sir.

PETRUCHIO
She will not lye yet, though she steal.

WHORE
A plain whore,
If you please to imploy me.

DUKE
And an impudent—

WHORE
Plain dealing now is impudence.
One, if you will Sir, can shew ye as much sport
In one half hour, and with as much variety,
As a far wiser woman can in half a year:
For there my way lies.

DUKE
Is she not drunk too?

WHORE
A little guilded o're Sir,
Old sack, old sack boys.

PETRUCHIO
This is saliant.

DON JOHN
A brave bold quean.

DUKE
Is this your certainty?
Do ye know the man ye wrong thus, Gentlemen?
Is this the woman meant?

FREDERICK
No.

DUKE
That your Land-lady?

DON JOHN
I know not what to say.

DUKE
Am I a person
To be your sport, Gentlemen?

DON JOHN
I do believe now certain
I am a knave; but how, or when—

DUKE
What are you?

PETRUCHIO
Bawd to this piece of pye meat.

BAWD
A poor Gentlewoman
That lyes in Town, about Law business,
And't like your worships.

PETRUCHIO
You shall have Law, believe it.

BAWD
I'le shew your Mastership my case.

PETRUCHIO
By no means,
I had rather see a Custard.

BAWD
My dead Husband
Left it even thus Sir.

DON JOHN
Bless mine eyes from blasting,
I was never so frighted with a case.

BAWD
And so Sir—

PETRUCHIO
Enough, put up good velvet head.

DUKE
What are you two now,
By your own free confessions?

FREDERICK
What you shall think us,
Though to my self I am certain, and my life
Shall make that good and perfect, or fall with it.

DON JOHN
We are sure of nothing, Fred, that's the truth on't:
I do not think my name's Don John, nor dare not
Believe any thing that concerns me, but my debts,
Nor those in way of payment: things are so carried,
What to entreat your grace, or how to tell ye
We are, or we are not, is past my cunning,
But I would fain imagine we are honest,
And o' my conscience, I should fight in't—

DUKE
Thus then,
For we may be all abus'd.

PETRUCHIO
'Tis possible,
For how should this concern them?

DUKE
Here let's part—
Until to morrow this time: we to our way,
To make this doubt out, and you to your way;
Pawning our honours then to meet again,
When if she be not found.

FREDERICK
We stand engaged
To answer any worthy way we are call'd to.

DUKE
We ask no more.

WHORE
Ye have done with us then?

PETRUCHIO
No, Dame.

DUKE
But is her name Constantia?

PETRUCHIO
Yes a moveable
Belonging to a friend of mine: come out Fidler,
What say you to this Lady? be not fearfull.

FRANCISCO
Saving the reverence of my Masters pleasure,
I say she is a whore, and that she has robb'd him,
Hoping his hurts would kill him.

WHORE
Who provok't me?
Nay Sirrah squeak, I'le see your treble strings
Ty'd up too; if I hang, I'le spoil your piping,
Your sweet face shall not save ye.

PETRUCHIO
Thou damn'd impudence,
And thou dry'd Devil; where's the officer?

OFFICER
He's here Sir.

[Enter **OFFICER**.

PETRUCHIO
Lodge these safe, till I send for 'em;
Let none come to 'em, nor no noise be heard
Of where they are, or why: away.

DON JOHN
By this hand
A handsom whore: Now will I be arrested,
And brought home to this officers: a stout whore,
I love such stirring ware: pox o' this business,
A man must hunt out morsels for another,
And starve himself: a quick-ey'd whore, that's wild-fire,
And makes the bloud dance through the veins like billows.
I will reprieve this whore.

DUKE
Well, good luck with ye.

FREDERICK
As much attend your grace.

PETRUCHIO
To morrow certain—

DON JOHN
If we out-live this night Sir.

FREDERICK
Come Don John,
We have something now to do.

DON JOHN
I am sure I would have.

FREDERICK
If she be not found, we must fight.

DON JOHN
I am glad on't,
I have not fought a great while.

FREDERICK
If we dye—

DON JOHN
There's so much mony sav'd in lecherie.

[Exeunt.

ACTUS QUINTUS

SCÆNA PRIMA

Enter **DUKE**, **PETRUCHIO**, below, and **VECCHIO**, above.

DUKE
It should be hereabouts.

PETRUCHIO
Your grace is right,
This is the house, I know it.

VECCHIO
Grace?

DUKE

'Tis further
By the description we received.

PETRUCHIO
Good my Lord the Duke,
Believe me, for I know it certainly,
This is the very house.

VECCHIO
My Lord the Duke?

DUKE
Pray Heaven this man prove right now.

PETRUCHIO
Believe it, he's a most sufficient Scholar,
And can do rare tricks this way; for a figure,
Or raising an appearance, whole Christendom
Has not a better; I have heard strange wonders of him.

DUKE
But can he shew us where she is?

PETRUCHIO
Most certain,
And for what cause too she departed.

DUKE
Knock then,
For I am great with expectation,
Till this man satisfie me: I fear the Spaniards,
Yet they appear brave fellows: can he tell us?

PETRUCHIO
With a wet finger, whether they be false.

DUKE
Away then.

PETRUCHIO
Who's within here?

[Enter **VECCHIO**.

VECCHIO
Your grace may enter.

DUKE

How can he know me?

PETRUCHIO
He knows all.

VECCHIO
And you Sir.

[Exeunt.

Enter **DON JOHN** and **FREDERICK**.

DON JOHN
What do you call his name?

FREDERICK
Why, Peter Vecchio.

DON JOHN
They say he can raise Devils,
Can he make 'em
Tell truth too, when he has rais'd 'em? for believe it,
These Devils are the lyingst Rascals.

FREDERICK
He can compel 'em.

DON JOHN
With what? can he
Tye squibs in their tails, and fire the truth out?
Or make 'em eat a bawling Puritan,
Whose sanctified zeal shall rumble like an Earth-quake?

FREDERICK
With Spells man.

DON JOHN
I with spoons as soon, dost thou think
The Devil such an Asse as people make him?
Such a poor coxcomb? such a penny foot-post?
Compel'd with cross and pile to run of errands?
With Asteroth, and Behemoth, and Belfagor?
Why should he shake at sounds, that lives in a smiths forge?
Or if he do—

FREDERICK
Without all doubt he do's John.

DON JOHN
Why should not Bilbo raise him, or a pair of bullyons,
They go as big as any? or an unshod Car,
When he goes tumble, tumble o're the stones,
Like Anacreons drunken verses, make us tremble?
These make as fell a noise; me thinks the colick
Well handled, and fed with small beer—

FREDERICK
'Tis the vertue—

DON JOHN
The vertue? nay, and goodness fetch him up once,
H'as lost a friend of me; the wise old Gentleman
Knows when, and how; I'le lay this hand to two pence,
Let all the Conjurers in Christendom,
With all their spells, and vertues call upon him,
And I but think upon a wench, and follow it,
He shall be sooner mine than theirs; where's vertue?

FREDERICK
Thou art the most sufficient, (I'le say for thee)
Not to believe a thing—

DON JOHN
O Sir, slow credit
Is the best child of knowledge; I'le go with ye,
And if he can do any thing, I'le think
As you would have me.

FREDERICK
Let's enquire along,
For certain we are not far off.

DON JOHN
Nor much nearer.

[Exeunt.

SCÆNA TERTIA

Enter **DUKE**, **PETRUCHIO** and **VECCHIO**.

VECCHIO
You lost her yester-night.

PETER
How think you Sir?

DUKE
Is your name Vecchio?

VECCHIO
Yes Sir.

DUKE
And you can shew me
These things you promise.

VECCHIO
Your graces word bound to me,
No hand of Law shall seize me.

DUKE
As I live Sir—

PETRUCHIO
And as I live, that can do something too Sir.

VECCHIO
I take your promises: stay here a little,
Till I prepare some Ceremonies, and I'le satisfie ye.
The Ladies name's Constantia?

PETRUCHIO
Yes.

VECCHIO
I come straight.

[Exit **VECCHIO**.

DUKE
Sure he's a learned man.

PETRUCHIO
The most now living;
Did your grace mark when we told all these circumstances,
How ever and anon he bolted from us
To use his studies help?

DUKE
Now I think rather
To talk with some familiar.

PETRUCHIO
Not unlikely,
For sure he has 'em subject.

DUKE
How could he else
Tell when she went, and who went with her?

PETRUCHIO
True.

DUKE
Or hit upon mine honour: or assure me
The Lady lov'd me dearly?

[Enter **VECCHIO**, in his habiliments.

PETRUCHIO
'Twas so.

VECCHIO
Now,
I do beseech your grace sit down, and you Sir;
Nay pray sit close like Brothers.

PETRUCHIO
A rare fellow.

VECCHIO
And what ye see, stir not at, nor use a word,
Until I ask ye; for what shall appear
Is but weak apparition and thin air,
Not to be held, nor spoken to.

[Knocking within.

[**DON JOHN, FREDERICK** and a **SERVANT** within.

DUKE
We are counsell'd—

VECCHIO
What noise is that without there?

FREDERICK
within. We must speak with him.

SERVANT
within. He's busie, Gentlemen.

DON JOHN [within]
That's all one friend,
We must and will speak with him.

DUKE
Let 'em in, Sir,
We know their tongues and business, 'tis our own,
And in this very cause that we now come for,
They also come to be instructed.

VECCHIO
Let 'em in then:
Sit down, I know your meaning.

[Enter **FREDERICK**, **DON JOHN**, and **SERVANT**.

FREDERICK
The Duke before us?
Now we shall sure know something.

VECCHIO
Not a question,
But make your Eyes your Tongues—

DON JOHN
This is a strange Jugler,
Neither indent before-hand for his payment,
Nor know the Breadth of the business; sure his Devil
Comes out of Lapland, where they sell men Winds
For dead drink, and old Doublets.

FREDERICK
Peace, he conjures.

DON JOHN
Let him, he cannot raise my Devil.

FREDERICK
Prithee Peace.

VECCHIO

Appear, appear,
And you soft Winds so clear,
That dance upon the leaves, and make them sing
Gentle Love-lays to the Spring,
Gilding all the Vales below,
With your Verdure as ye blow,
Raise these forms from under ground
With a soft and happy sound.

[Soft Musick.

DON JOHN
This is an honest Conjurer, and a pretty Poet;
I like his words well, there's no bumbast in 'em,
But do you think now he can cudgel up the Devil
With this short Staff of Verses?

FREDERICK
Peace, the Spirits—

[**TWO SHAPES** of women passing by.

DON JOHN
Nay, and they be no worse—

VECCHIO
Do ye know these faces?

DUKE
No.

VECCHIO
Sit still upon your lives then, and mark what follows;
Away, away.

DON JOHN
These Devils do not paint sure?
Have they no sweeter shapes in Hell?

FREDERICK
Hark now, **DON JOHN**

[**CONSTANTIA** passes by.

DON JOHN
I, marry, this moves something like, this Devil
Carries some metal in her gate.

VECCHIO
I find ye,
You would see her face unvail'd?

DUKE
Yes.

VECCHIO
Be uncovered.

DUKE
O Heaven!

VECCHIO
Peace.

PETER
See how she blushes.

DON JOHN
Frederick,
This Devil for my mony; this is she, Boy,
Why dost thou shake? I burn.

VECCHIO
Sit still, and silent.

DUKE
She looks back at me, now she smiles, Sir.

VECCHIO
Silence.

DUKE
I must rise, or I burst.

[Exit **CONSTANTIA**.

VECCHIO
Ye see what follows—

DUKE
O gentle Sir, this shape agen.

VECCHIO
I cannot.
'Tis all dissolv'd again; this was the Figure?

DUKE
The very same, Sir.
No hope once more to see it?

VECCHIO
You might have kept it longer, had ye spar'd it,
Now 'tis impossible.

DUKE
No means to find it?

VECCHIO
Yes, that there is, sit still a while, there's Wine
To thaw the wonder from your hearts; drink well, Sir.

[Exit **VECCHIO**.

DON JOHN
This Conjurer is a right good fellow too,
A Lad of mettle; two such Devils more
Would make me a Conjurer; what wine is it?

FREDERICK
Hollock.

DON JOHN
The Devil's in it then; look how it dances.
Well, if I be—

PETER
We are all before ye,
That's your best comfort, Sir.

DON JOHN
By th' Mass, brave Wine;
Nay, and the Devils live in this Hell, I dare venture
Within these two months yet to be delivered
Of a large Legion of 'em.

[Enter **VECCHIO**.

DUKE
Here he comes,
Silence of all sides, Gentlemen.

VECCHIO
Good your Grace,
Observe a stricter temper, and you too, Gallants,

You'll be deluded all else. This merry Devil
That next appears, for such a one you'll find it,
Must be call'd up by a strange incantation,
A Song, and I must sing it: 'pray bear with me,
And pardon my rude Pipe; for yet, ere parting
Twenty to one I please ye.

DUKE
We are arm'd, Sir.

PETER
Nor shall you see us more transgress.

FREDERICK
What think'st thou
Now, John?

DON JOHN
Why, now do I think, Frederick,
(And if I think amiss Heaven pardon me)
This honest Conjurer, with some four or five
Of his good fellow Devils, and my self,
Shall be yet drunk ere midnight.

SONG.
Come away, thou Lady gay,
Hoist; how she stumbles!
Hark how she mumbles.
Dame Gillian. Answer. I come, I come.
By old Claret I enlarge thee,
By Canary thus I charge thee,
By Britain, Mathewglin, and Peeter,
Appear and answer me in meeter.
Why when?
Why Gill?
Why when?
Answer. You'll tarry till I am ready.
Once again I conjure thee,
By the Pose in thy Nose,
And the Gout in thy Toes;
By thine old dryed Skin,
And the Mummie within;
By thy little, little Ruff,
And thy Hood that's made of Stuff;
By thy Bottle at thy Breech,
And thine old salt Itch;
By the Stakes, and the Stones,
That have worn out thy Bones.

Appear.
Appear.
Appear.
Answer. Oh I am here.

FREDERICK
Peace, he conjures.

DON JOHN
Why, this is the Song, Frederick; twenty pound now,
To see but our Don Gillian.

[Enter **LANDLADY** and the **CHILD**.

FREDERICK
Peace, it appears.

DON JOHN
I cannot peace; Devils in French hoods, Frederick?
Satans old Syringes?

DUKE
What's this?

VECCHIO
Peace.

DON JOHN
She, Boy.

FREDERICK
What dost thou mean?

DON JOHN
She, Boy, I say.

FREDERICK
Ha?

DON JOHN
She Boy,
The very Child too, Frederick.

FREDERICK
She laughs on us
Aloud, John, has the Devil these affections?
I do believe 'tis she, indeed.

VECCHIO
Stand still.

DON JOHN
I will not;
Who calls Jeronimo from his naked Bed?
Sweet Lady, was it you? if thou beest the Devil,
First, having crost my self, to keep out wildfire,
Then said some special Prayers to defend me
Against thy most unhallowed Hood, have at thee.

LANDLADY
Hold, Sir, I am no Devil.

DON JOHN
That's all one.

LANDLADY
I am your very Landlady.

DON JOHN
I defie thee;
Thus as St. Dunstan blew the Devil's Nose
With a pair of tongs, even so, Right Worshipful—

LANDLADY
Sweet Son, I am old Gillian.

DUKE
This is no Spirit.

DON JOHN
Art thou old Gillian, flesh and bone?

LANDLADY
I am, Son.

VECCHIO
Sit still, Sir, now I'll shew you all.

[Exit **VECCHIO**

DON JOHN
Where's thy Bottle?

LANDLADY
Here, I beseech ye, Son—

DON JOHN
For I know the Devil
Cannot assume that shape.

FREDERICK
'Tis she, John, certain—

DON JOHN
A hogs pox o' your mouldy chaps, what makes you
Tumbling and juggling here?

LANDLADY
I am quit now, Seignior,
For all the pranks you plaid, and railings at me,
For to tell true, out of a trick I put
Upon your high behaviours, which was a lie,
But then it serv'd my turn, I drew the Lady
Unto my Kinsman's here, only to torture
Your Don-ships for a day or two; and secure her
Out of all thoughts of danger; here she comes now.

[Enter **VECCHIO**, and **CONSTANTIA**.

DUKE
May I yet speak?

VECCHIO
Yes, and embrace her too,
For one that loves you dearer—

DUKE
O my Sweetest.

PETER
Blush not, I will not chide ye.

CONSTANTIA
To add more
Unto the joy I know, I bring ye, see Sir,
The happy fruit of all our Vows!

DUKE
Heavens Blessing
Be round about thee ever.

DON JOHN
Pray bless me too,
For if your Grace be well instructed this way,

You'll find the keeping half the getting.

DUKE
How, Sir?

DON JOHN
I'll tell you that anon.

CONSTANTIA
'Tis true, this Gentleman
Has done a charity worthy your favour,
And let him have it, dear Sir.

DUKE
My best Lady
He has, and ever shall have: so must you, Sir,
To whom I am equal bound as to my being.

FREDERICK
Your Graces humble servant—

DUKE
Why kneel you, Sir?

VECCHIO
For pardon for my boldness: yet 'twas harmless,
And all the art I have, Sir; those your Grace saw,
Which you thought spirits, were my Neighbours Children
Whom I instruct in Grammar here, and Musick;
Their shapes, the Peoples fond opinions,
Believing I can conjure, and oft repairing
To know of things stoln from 'em, I keep about me,
And always have in readiness, by conjecture
Out of their own confessions, I oft tell 'em
Things that by chance have fallen out so; which way
(Having the persons here, I knew you sought for)
I wrought upon your Grace; my end is mirth,
And pleasing, if I can, all parties.

DUKE
I believe it,
For you have pleas'd me truly: so well pleas'd me,
That when I shall forget it—

PETER
Here's old Antonio,
I spy'd him at a window, coming mainly
I know about his Whore, the man you light on,

As you discovered unto me; good your Grace,
Let's stand by all, 'twill be a mirth above all,
To observe his pelting fury.

VECCHIO
About a wench, Sir?

PETER
A young whore that has rob'd him.

VECCHIO
But do you know, Sir,
Where she is?

PETER
Yes, and will make that perfect—

VECCHIO
I am instructed well then.

DON JOHN
If he come
To have a Devil shew'd him, by all means
Let me be he, I can roar rarely.

PETER
Be so,
But take heed to his anger.

VECCHIO
Slip in quickly,
There you shall find suits of all sorts: when I call
Be ready and come forward.

[Exeunt all but **VECCHIO**.

Who's there comes in?

[Enter **ANTONIO**.

ANTONIO
Are you the Conjurer?

VECCHIO
Sir, I can do a little
That way, if you please to employ me.

ANTONIO

Presently, shew me a Devil that can tell—

VECCHIO
Where your wench is.

ANTONIO
You are i'th' right; as also where the Fidler
That was consenting to her.

VECCHIO
Sit ye there, Sir,
Ye shall know presently: can ye pray heartily?

ANTONIO
Why, is your Devil so furious?

VECCHIO
I must shew ye
A form may chance affright ye.

ANTONIO
He must fart fire then:
Take you no care for me.

VECCHIO
Ascend, Asterth,

[Enter **DON JOHN** like a Spirit.

Why, when, appear I say—Now question him.

ANTONIO
Where is my whore, Don Devil?

DON JOHN
Gone to China,
To be the great Chams Mistress.

ANTONIO
That's a lye, Devil,
Where are my jewels?

DON JOHN
Pawn'd for Petticoats.

ANTONIO
That may be: where's the Fidler?

DON JOHN
Condemn'd to th' Gallows
For robbing of a Mill.

ANTONIO
The lyingst Devil
That e'r I dealt withal, and the unlikeliest!
What was that Rascal hurt me?

DON JOHN
I.

ANTONIO
How?

DON JOHN
I.

ANTONIO
Who was he?

DON JOHN
I.

ANTONIO
Do you hear conjurer,
Dare you venture your Devil?

VECCHIO
Yes.

ANTONIO
Then I'll venture my dagger;
Have at your Devils pate; do you mew?

[Enter **ALL**.

VECCHIO
Hold.

PETER
Hold there,
I do command you hold.

ANTONIO
Is this the Devil?
Why, Conjurer—

PETER
He has been a Devil to you, Sir;
But now you shall forget all; your whore's safe,
And all your jewels, your Boy too.

DON JOHN
Now the Devil indeed
Lay his ten claws upon thee, for my pate
Finds what it is to be a Fiend.

ANTONIO
All safe?

PETER
'Pray ye know this person; all's right now.

ANTONIO
Your Grace
May now command me then: but where's my whore?

PETER
Ready to go to whipping.

ANTONIO
My whore whipt?

PETER
Yes, your whore without doubt, Sir.

ANTONIO
Whipt! 'pray Gentlemen.

DUKE
Why, would you have her once more rob ye? the young Boy
You may forgive, he was entic'd.

DON JOHN
The whore, Sir,
Would rather carry pity: a handsome whore.

ANTONIO
A Gentleman I warrant thee.

PETER
Let's in all,
And if we see contrition in your whore, Sir,
Much may be done.

DUKE
Now my dear fair to you,
And the full consummation of my Vow.

[Exeunt.

EPILOGUE

We have not held you long, nor do I see
One Brow in this selected Companie
Assuring a dislike, our Pains were eas'd
Could we be confident that all rise pleas'd:
But such ambition soars too high; If We
Have satisfi'd the best, and they agree
In a fair Censure, We have our Reward,
And in them arm'd desire no surer Guard.

John Fletcher – A Short Biography

John Fletcher was born in December, 1579 in Rye, Sussex. He was baptised on December 20th.

As can be imagined details of much of his life and career have not survived and, accordingly, only a very brief indication of his life and works can be given.

His father, Richard Fletcher, was a successful and rather ambitious cleric. From being the Dean of Peterborough he moved on to become the Bishop of Bristol, Bishop of Worcester and finally, shortly before his death, the Bishop of London. He was also the chaplain to Queen Elizabeth.

When he was Dean of Peterborough, Richard Fletcher, witnessed the execution of Mary, Queen of Scots. It was said he "knelt down on the scaffold steps and started to pray out loud and at length, in a prolonged and rhetorical style, as though determined to force his way into the pages of history". He cried out at her death, "So perish all the Queen's enemies!" All very dramatic but the family did have strong links to the Arts.

Young Fletcher appears at the very young age of eleven to have entered Corpus Christi College at Cambridge University in 1591. There are no records that he ever took a degree but there is some small evidence that he was being prepared for a career in the church.

However what is clear is that this was soon abandoned as he joined the stream of people who would leave University and decamp to the more bohemian life of commercial theatre in London.

Unfortunately his father fell out with Queen Elizabeth but appears to have been on his way to rehabilitation before his death in 1596. At his death he was, however, mired in debt.

The upbringing of the now teenage Fletcher and his seven siblings now passed to his paternal uncle, the poet and minor official Giles Fletcher. Giles, who had the patronage of the Earl of Essex may have been a liability rather than an advantage to the young Fletcher. With Essex involved in the failed rebellion against Elizabeth Giles was also tainted by association.

By 1606 John Fletcher appears to have equipped himself with the talents to become a playwright. Initially this appears to have been for the Children of the Queen's Revels, then performing at the Blackfriars Theatre.

Commendatory verses by Richard Brome in the Beaumont and Fletcher 1647 folio place Fletcher in the company of Ben Jonson, although it is not known when this friendship began. Jonson, of course, was a leviathan of English Literature, so admired that many of his literary friends and colleagues were simply known as 'Sons of Ben'. Fletcher's frequent early collaborator, Francis Beaumont, was also a friend of Jonson's.

Fletcher's early career was marked by one significant failure; The Faithful Shepherdess, his adaptation of Giovanni Battista Guarini's Il Pastor Fido, which was performed by the Blackfriars Children in 1608. In the preface to the printed edition of his play, Fletcher explained the failure as due to his audience's faulty expectations. They expected a pastoral tragicomedy to feature dances, comedy, and murder, with the shepherds presented in conventional stereotypes – as Fletcher put it, wearing "gray cloaks, with curtailed dogs in strings." Fletcher's preface is however best known for its pithy definition of tragicomedy: "A tragicomedy is not so called in respect of mirth and killing, but in respect it wants [i.e., lacks] deaths, which is enough to make it no tragedy; yet brings some near it, which is enough to make it no comedy." A comedy, he went on to say, must be "a representation of familiar people." His preface is critical of drama that features characters whose action violates nature.

In that case, Fletcher appears to have been developing a new style faster than audiences could comprehend. By 1609, however, he had found his stride. With Beaumont, he wrote Philaster, which became a hit for the King's Men and began a profitable association between Fletcher and that company. Philaster appears also to have begun a trend for tragicomedy. Fletcher's influence has also been said to have inspired some features of Shakespeare's late romances, and certainly his influence on the tragicomic work of other playwrights is even more marked.

By the middle of the 1610s, Fletcher's plays had achieved a popularity that rivalled Shakespeare's and cemented the pre-eminence of the King's Men in Jacobean London. After Beaumont's retirement, necessitated by ill-health, and then his early death in 1616, Fletcher continued working, both singly and in collaboration, until his death in 1625. By that time, he had produced, or had been credited with, close to fifty plays. This body of work remained a major part of the King's Men's repertory until the closing of the theatres in 1642 due to the Civil War.

At the beginning of his career Fletcher's most important collaborator was Francis Beaumont. The two wrote together for close to a decade, first for the Children of the Queen's Revels, and then for the King's Men. According to an anecdote transmitted or invented by John Aubrey, they also lived together in Bankside, sharing clothes and having "one wench in the house between them." This domestic arrangement, if it existed, was ended by Beaumont's marriage in 1613, and their dramatic partnership ended after Beaumont fell ill, probably of a stroke, that same year.

At this point Fletcher had written many plays with Beaumont and several others on his own. He seems to have been regarded as quite a talent although it should be remembered that playwrights were required to be prolific, to easily work with other collaborators and to produce work of quality and commercial appeal very quickly.

The King's Men, run by Philip Henslowe, was the most prestigious of the theatre companies and Fletcher now had an increasingly close association with it.

Fletcher collaborated with Shakespeare on Henry VIII, The Two Noble Kinsmen, and the now lost Cardenio, which some scholars say was the basis for Lewis Theobald's play Double Falsehood. (Theobald is regarded as one of the best Shakespearean editors. Whether his play is based on Cardenio or on some other is not absolutely known although Theobald certainly promoted it as his revision of the lost Shakespeare/Fletcher play.)

A play that Fletcher also wrote by himself at this time, The Woman's Prize or the Tamer Tamed, is also regarded as a sequel to The Taming of the Shrew.

In 1616, with the death of Shakespeare, Fletcher now appears to have entered into an enhanced arrangement with the King's Men on very similar terms to Shakespeare's. Fletcher would now write exclusively for the King's Men until his own death almost a decade later.

As well as continuing his solo productions Fletcher was still collaborating with other playwrights, mainly Philip Massinger, who, in turn, would succeed him as the in-house playwright for the King's Men.

Fletcher's popularity continued throughout his life; indeed during the winter of 1621, he had three of his plays performed at court. His mastery is most notable in two dramatic types; tragicomedy and the comedy of manners.

John Fletcher died in 1625, it is thought of bubonic plague which, at the time, was undergoing further outbreaks.

He seems to have been buried in what is now Southwark Cathedral, although a precise location is not known. There is much made of an anecdote that Fletcher and Massinger (who died in 1640) share the same grave but it is more likely that both are buried within a few yards of each other and that the stone markers in the floor have confused the issue. One is marked 'Edmond Shakespeare 1607' and the other 'John Fletcher 1625' refers to Shakespeare's younger brother and the playwright. The churchyards were, more often than not, completely over-crowded and breeding grounds for disease. Precise record keeping was not a practiced skill.

During the later Commonwealth, many of the playwright's best-known scenes were kept alive as drolls. These were brief performances, usually condensed into one or two scenes and with the addition of music or song to satisfy the taste for plays while the theatres were closed under the Puritans. At the re-opening of the theatres in 1660, the plays in the Fletcher canon, in original form or revised, were by far the most common productions on the English stage. The most frequently revived plays suggest the developing taste for comedies of manners. Among the tragedies, The Maid's Tragedy and, especially, Rollo Duke of Normandy held the stage. Four tragicomedies (A King and No King, The Humorous Lieutenant, Philaster, and The Island Princess) were popular, perhaps in part for their similarity to and foreshadowing of heroic drama. Four comedies (Rule a Wife And Have a Wife, The Chances, Beggars' Bush, and especially The Scornful Lady) were also stage mainstays.

Despite his popularity, and it appears he was held in higher regard than Shakespeare at this time, his works steadily lost ground to those of Shakespeare and to new productions from other playwrights.

Since then Fletcher has increasingly become a subject only for occasional revivals and for specialists. Fletcher and his collaborators have been the subject of important bibliographic and critical studies, but the plays have been revived only infrequently.

Due to the frequent collaborations between all manner of playwrights, and the revisions carried out in later years, having a settled list of authorship to any given set of plays can be problematic. The works of Fletcher and others of this period most definitely fall into this category. It is as well to take into account that during this period theatres were quite often closed either due to outbreaks of the plague or to the prevailing political and moral climate. Printers, anxious to provide materials that would sell, were not above changing a name or two to enhance sales.

Although Fletcher collaborated most often with Beaumont and Massinger, it is believed that Massinger revised many of the plays some time after their original production. Other collaborators including Nathan Field, William Shakespeare, William Rowley and others also can be seen distinctly in Fletchers' works. Many modern scholars point out that Fletcher had many particular mannerisms but other playwrights would also duplicate these at times so allocating exact contributions of anyone to a play is somewhat of a detective case in many instances. However from the original folio printings or licensing via the Master of the Revels (the statutory licensing authority to approve and censor plays as well a hand in publication and printing of theatrical materials) as well as contemporary notes a fairly precise bibliography of the works can be given with only a few plays lacking substantial authority and provenance.

John Fletcher – A Concise Bibliography

This bibliography gives the most likely date of writing together with when published, revised or licensed by the Master or the Revels (This position within the royal household was originally for royal festivities, ie revels, and later to oversee stage censorship, until this function was transferred to the Lord Chamberlain in 1624).

Solo Plays
The Faithful Shepherdess, pastoral (written 1608–9; printed 1609)
The Tragedy of Valentinian, tragedy (1610–14; 1647)
Monsieur Thomas, comedy (c. 1610–16; 1639)
The Woman's Prize, or The Tamer Tamed, comedy (c. 1611; 1647)
Bonduca, tragedy (1611–14; 1647)
The Chances, comedy (c. 1613–25; 1647)
Wit Without Money, comedy (c. 1614; 1639)
The Mad Lover, tragicomedy (acted 5 January 1617; 1647)
The Loyal Subject, tragicomedy (licensed 16 November 1618; revised 1633; 1647)
The Humorous Lieutenant, tragicomedy (c. 1619; 1647)

Women Pleased, tragicomedy (c. 1619–23; 1647)
The Island Princess, tragicomedy (c. 1620; 1647)
The Wild Goose Chase, comedy (c. 1621; 1652)
The Pilgrim, comedy (c. 1621; 1647)
A Wife for a Month, tragicomedy (licensed 27 May 1624; 1647)
Rule a Wife and Have a Wife, comedy (licensed 19 October 1624; 1640)

Collaborations

With Francis Beaumont
The Woman Hater, comedy (1606; 1607)
Cupid's Revenge, tragedy (c. 1607–12; 1615)
Philaster, or Love Lies a-Bleeding, tragicomedy (c. 1609; 1620)
The Maid's Tragedy, Tragedy (c. 1609; 1619)
A King and No King, tragicomedy (1611; 1619)
The Captain, comedy (c. 1609–12; 1647)
The Scornful Lady, comedy (c. 1613; 1616)
Love's Pilgrimage, tragicomedy (c. 1615–16; 1647)
The Noble Gentleman, comedy (c. 1613; licensed 3 February 1626; 1647)

With Francis Beaumont & Philip Massinger
Thierry & Theodoret, tragedy (c. 1607; 1621)
The Coxcomb, comedy (c. 1608–10; 1647)
Beggars' Bush, comedy (c. 1612–13; revised 1622; 1647)
Love's Cure, comedy (c. 1612–13; revised 1625; 1647)

With Philip Massinger
Sir John van Olden Barnavelt, tragedy (August 1619; MS)
The Little French Lawyer, comedy (c. 1619–23; 1647)
A Very Woman, tragicomedy (c. 1619–22; licensed 6 June 1634; 1655)
The Custom of the Country, comedy (c. 1619–23; 1647)
The Double Marriage, tragedy (c. 1619–23; 1647)
The False One, history (c. 1619–23; 1647)
The Prophetess, tragicomedy (licensed 14 May 1622; 1647)
The Sea Voyage, comedy (licensed 22 June 1622; 1647)
The Spanish Curate, comedy (licensed 24 October 1622; 1647)
The Lovers' Progress or The Wandering Lovers, tragicomedy (licensed 6 December 1623; rev 1634; 1647)
The Elder Brother, comedy (c. 1625; 1637)

With Philip Massinger & Nathan Field
The Honest Man's Fortune, tragicomedy (1613; 1647)
The Queen of Corinth, tragicomedy (c. 1616–18; 1647)
The Knight of Malta, tragicomedy (c. 1619; 1647)

With William Shakespeare
Henry VIII, history (c. 1613; 1623)
The Two Noble Kinsmen, tragicomedy (c. 1613; 1634)

Cardenio, tragicomedy (c. 1613)

With Thomas Middleton & William Rowley
Wit at Several Weapons, comedy (c. 1610–20; 1647)

With William Rowley
The Maid in the Mill (licensed 29 August 1623; 1647).

With Nathan Field
Four Plays, or Moral Representations, in One, morality (c. 1608–13; 1647)

With Philip Massinger, Ben Jonson and George Chapman
Rollo Duke of Normandy, or The Bloody Brother, tragedy (c. 1617; revised 1627–30; 1639)

With James Shirley
The Night Walker, or The Little Thief, comedy (c. 1611; 1640)
The Coronation c. 1635

Uncertain
The Nice Valour, or The Passionate Madman, comedy (c. 1615–25; 1647)
The Laws of Candy, tragicomedy (c. 1619–23; 1647)
The Fair Maid of the Inn, comedy (licensed 22 January 1626; 1647)
The Faithful Friends, tragicomedy (registered 29 June 1660; MS.)

The Nice Valour is possibly by Fletcher revised by Thomas Middleton;

The Fair Maid of the Inn is perhaps a play by Massinger, John Ford, and John Webster, either with or without Fletcher's involvement.

The Laws of Candy has been variously attributed to Fletcher and to John Ford.

The Night-Walker was a Fletcher original, with additions by Shirley for a 1639 production.

Even now there is not absolute certainty on several of the plays. The first Beaumont & Fletcher folio of 1647 contained 35 plays and the second folio of 1679 added a further 18. In total 53 plays.

The first folio included The Masque of the Inner Temple and Gray's Inn (1613), and the second The Knight of the Burning Pestle (1607), widely considered Beaumont's solo works, although the latter was in early editions attributed to both writers. Fletcher himself said that Beaumont was attributed so-authorship of many works that belonged solely to Fletcher or to other collaborators.

One play in the canon, Sir John Van Olden Barnavelt, existed in manuscript and was not published till 1883.

www.ingramcontent.com/pod-product-compliance
Lightning Source LLC
Chambersburg PA
CBHW060117050426
42448CB00010B/1912